Testimonials...

"A compelling, insightful and practical guide on leadership. Drawing on wisdom from historical figures, leadership experts and the author's personal experiences, it is a call to action for leadership in the 21st century. Phillip has done a great job of not only synthesising the latest in leadership theory but adding new and practical insights that will assist anyone who is passionate about their own leadership journey or making a difference in their places of work."

Mark Priede
Head of Culture Strategy (Australia)
National Australia Bank

"Engaging style, easy to read, great mix of theory and live experience. Philip Ralph has written a practical handbook for leaders who want to dig deeper, and transform themselves and their organisations. Courage required. Faint-hearted types advised to steer clear of this book."

Phil Clothier
Chief Executive Officer
Barrett Values Centre, United Kingdom

"*Leadership Without Silver Bullets* is a must read for anyone who seeks to be a successful leader in today's world in any capacity, whether in an organisation or the community. Phillip Ralph exposes some of the flaws in traditional leadership thinking and offers a fresh paradigm which calls us all to respond differently to the adaptive challenges we face. The book provides a practical model to use to develop leadership at all levels of an organisation."

John Fogarty
Chief Executive Officer
St John of God Hospital (Ballarat), Australia

LEADERSHIP

Without

SILVER BULLETS

LEADERSHIP

Without

SILVER BULLETS:

A Guide to Exercising Leadership

Phillip Ralph

Leadership Without Silver Bullets:
A Guide to Exercising Leadership

Phillip Ralph

www.theleadershipsphere.com.au

iUniverse books may be ordered through booksellers or by contacting:

iUniverse
1663 Liberty Drive
Bloomington, IN 47403
www.iuniverse.com
1-800-Authors (1-800-288-4677)

Order copies at: www.leadershipwithoutsilverbullets.com.au

Ralph, Phillip
Leadership Without Silver Bullets: A Guide to Exercising Leadership
1st ed.

ISBN: 978-1-4502-2815-2 (sc)
ISBN: 978-1-4502-2816-9 (e)

1. Leadership development. 2. High Performance 3. Organisational development 4. Leadership development

Printed in the United States of America

iUniverse rev. date: 06/14/2011

To those who choose to lead

Contents

Foreword

Does the world really need another book about leadership? A quick trip to the local bookstore reveals we are almost drowning in a sea of literature on the subject. The majority peddle a variation of the "Great Man" theory of leadership: leadership is for those special individuals born with a rare and mythical set of qualities who step forward at the right moment with the right answer. Some offer an easy path – follow a few quick, easy steps and you too can have what it takes to be a great leader. Many are simply management tools – worthwhile but distinct from the leadership question. Plenty of leadership *with* silver bullets! Frankly, most of these books are not very helpful to anyone serious about exercising leadership on tough, complex challenges in the 21st century.

Phillip Ralph's *Leadership Without Silver Bullets* offers a refreshing antidote to this plethora of stale or simplistic notions of leadership. Phil approaches the topic with an unusual combination of clarity, honesty and insightfulness. Through the story of his leadership journey, Phil shares his own struggle, the lessons and personal transformation that enabled him to see the world differently, reframing leadership from something mythical and elitist to an accessible activity with the potential to transform our organisations and our world.

Reading *Leadership Without Silver Bullets* reminded me of a wonderful quote from Oliver Wendell Holmes:

I would not give a fig for the simplicity this side of complexity. I would, however, give my life for the simplicity on the other side of complexity.

Phil explores the complexity of leadership with a simplicity that allows the reader to access the wisdom borne out of years of hard practice and learning – not a false simplicity offering trite answers or solutions, but a simplicity borne out of years of the "hard yakka" of teaching and consulting in tough, complex environments combined with deep thinking and reflection.

Phillip possesses another great quality, again sorely lacking in much leadership literature, namely, humility. His writing, like his practice, lacks ego. His words serve the readers' needs and learning. Having had the privilege and pleasure of working alongside Phil in a classroom setting, I have observed his careful, understated and skilful approach. Like all great practitioners in any realm, it looks effortless but reveals someone who knows their craft and is able to serve a greater purpose. He is not afraid to challenge our assumptions, thinking and behaviour, but does this without arrogance or censure.

At the core of his work is a deep love of learning and a profound curiosity. He is equally able to learn from his own children as from CEOs he has coached, or some of the leading thinkers and intellectuals of our times. They all have something to offer, to hear, and to learn from. He shares these insights with us like a generous gift.

So, do we really need another leadership book? When the book is as accessible, practical and wise as Phillip Ralph's *Leadership Without Silver Bullets,* the answer is a resounding "yes". I hope you agree and benefit from his shared knowledge and understanding.

Robbie Macpherson
Head
Social Leadership Australia (The Benevolent Society) Sydney, Australia

What people are saying about *Leadership Without Silver Bullets...*

"I have had the privilege of seeing the results of Phillip Ralph's work as a leadership coach. He is outstanding. I can highly recommend this book as both practical and inspiring with valuable insights on how leadership in organisations really works."

Michael Rennie
Managing Partner
McKinsey and Company, Australia and New Zealand

"This work exposes many of the myths about leadership and presents a very clear and practical guide to what *effective* leadership is really about. Any organisation would benefit by following the principles outlined to raise the bar on leadership and organisational performance."

Louis Hawke
Managing Director of Retail Distribution
Australia and New Zealand Banking Group Limited (ANZ), Melbourne, Australia

"Phillip has done a fine job in debunking the modern myths on leadership, whilst constructing an accessible and eminently applicable model for today's organisational challenges. He demonstrates that leadership is shared and it's fluid, and the best leaders are those who enable others to lead, at any level of the organisation. I commend this work to any who want to see real change and growth in themselves and their organisation."

Greg Camm
Chief Executive Officer
Superpartners, Melbourne, Australia

"This is not just another book claiming to deliver the secrets of leadership success. Instead, through the use of thought-provoking examples and practical ideas, Phillip shares his unique take on what defines real leaders. The Seven Spheres of Leadership Mastery model will clearly assist organisations and HR professionals by providing a platform and language for discussing leadership capability. It certainly has influenced the way in which I think about what makes a great leader."

Shaneen Argall
Director, Human Resources
SMS Management & Technology, Melbourne, Australia

"Phil has an amazing ability to quickly and succinctly help the reader get to grips with the world of leadership development, its history and its challenges. Where Phil has 'nailed it' is in his Leadership Declaration. This insight lets us understand that effective leadership is not just in the hands of a chosen few but rather we are all leaders in our own rights and can make a difference in our communities and businesses by applying a few simple but powerful techniques. Most importantly, it expresses the need for true leaders to be values-driven and to have the courage to do things differently. Underpinning his thinking are years of practical leadership development experience, robust models and the use of pragmatic examples that every leader can relate to."

Anthony Youds
Director
Crossroads Human Resources, Melbourne, Australia

"*Leadership Without Silver Bullets: A Guide to Exercising Leadership* is an informative read for anyone who leads a team and is seeking guidance on how to achieve employee engagement. Through personal experiences and straightforward analysis of recent leadership studies, this book reminds the reader of the modelling from school days to boardroom, which has led to the dominance of uninspiring, individualist, 'command-and-control' management styles. This thought-provoking book may well be the catalyst for readers to develop a shared leadership approach to allow their disempowered teams to flourish."

Erin Duncan
Learning & Development Manager
Merck, Sharp & Dohme, Sydney, Australia

"As the CEO of a children's charity determined to create a better world for children experiencing disadvantage, investment in our people is paramount. When our work is about making sure that vulnerable children have what they need and resources are limited, then it is imperative that we can actively unleash our collective capacity and wisdom to make a difference. *Leadership Without Silver Bullets* is an accessible read that inspires reflection and determination to be the kind of leader that not only brings out the best in everyone, but enables the change that we want to see in the world."

Mandy Burns
Chief Executive Officer
Ardoch Youth Foundation, Melbourne, Australia

"This book highlights and identifies some new and at times challenging thoughts on leadership which will have a positive impact on all who are courageous enough to not only read the book but implement some personal and team changes. Phil has drawn upon his deep experience in working in many different management and leadership roles during his working life. The stated aim of the book 'To inspire and ignite leadership action that makes a difference for you, your organisation and the world' particularly resonated. I believe current and aspiring leaders and managers should put this on their 'must-read' list."

Peter Callaway
Managing Director
RISQ, Melbourne, Australia

Preface

Whether corporations succeed or fail, we somehow usually end up talking about the *leader* and his or her *leadership*. These words are also often used whether *real leadership* is present or not. We often assign a role to the word "leader", rather than an action. Despite this, there seems to be almost a crisis of leadership identity. Am I a leader? What does that really mean anyway? For example, I've asked hundreds of groups (mostly executives and senior managers) what they think leadership means. I get almost as many answers as there are people in the room. I am also dismayed by the largely wasted expenditure on misguided leadership development. Sadly, *leadership* is perhaps the most overused and abused word in modern organisational language.

While this book is not about trying to settle the leadership score once-and-for-all by coming up with 'the one right view', it does aim to provide a fresh and useful perspective for you, the reader, whether you are a member of a board, a chief executive, executive, middle manager, HR professional, or someone who chooses to make a difference. While I would not claim to have invented a new paradigm (another overused word), my hope and intention is that my small contribution in this book and ongoing work builds on the emerging new paradigm in a meaningful way.

In Part 1, *Leadership Today and Why It's Not Working*, I will share with you some of the things that I and others have learnt trying to understand and navigate the often messy territory of leadership, whilst drawing on my twenty years plus journey working with literally thousands of leaders in dozens of different industries and roles. In Part 2, *Why Most Leaders Don't Lead*, I will present an argument on why I think we generally do not lead effectively and make the case that effective leadership is more important than ever before. In Part 3, *A Leadership Declaration – Our Vision for the Future*, I will present a fresh approach to leadership – one that provides more clarity and focus on where and how we need to develop leadership capability, irrespective of role or title. Finally, in Part 4, *The Seven Spheres of Leadership Mastery*, I will bring our Leadership Declaration to life through a 'rolling case study' and real-life examples. During this process, my hope is that you will take the opportunity to reflect on your own leadership and how it relates to who you are, your work and the world around you that you influence in some way every day.

By reading this book I hope that you become clear about the type of leadership that you need and want in your own organisation, and that your own leadership journey is enriched in a tangible way.

Phillip Ralph
Melbourne, Australia
April 2010

Acknowledgements

This book has really been written over the last two decades. It is the product of many experiences in many different contexts. During that time, learning and curiosity have been two core drivers of mine. Friends and family still wonder how I can read leadership literature in my "down time". My thirst for knowledge and understanding of leadership, team development and culture change continues unabated.

Over the years, I have worked with many truly amazing leaders, both when I was part of an organisation and also in a leadership consulting capacity. These men and women have inspired me to enhance my own leadership capability and to stretch myself in the work I now do with clients. The trust that clients put in me and my colleagues at The Leadership Sphere in supporting them to achieve breakthrough performance continues to be a humbling experience. I have also worked with many people I feel proud to call colleagues, many of whom are among my best friends and confidants. I thank you from the bottom of my heart for your support, growth and friendship.

I would especially like to thank Dr Greg Chapman for pushing me to write this book in the first place, along with numerous reviewers, including Kylie Italiano, Emma Laing and David Mills. Finally, a special thanks to my wife, Kerrie, and children, Thomas, Emma and Caitlin, for your love and support.

Part One:

Leadership Today and Why It's Not Working

Chapter 1

Introduction

The greatest obstacle to discovery is not ignorance
– it is the illusion of knowledge.

Daniel J. Boorstin *(1914 – 2004), American*
historian, professor, attorney, and writer.

Follow the Leader

At a very early age, I learned that the leader was the person out the front, showing everyone what they needed to do and where they needed to go. Like many young children I was taught a *game* at primary school called *follow-the-leader*. I dare say you were taught this exact same game, or perhaps a slight variation (does *Simon Says* ring a bell?). The game basically entailed a designated leader positioned out the front giving orders and demonstrating to others the required path and actions. The *followers* (in this case a group of rowdy five year olds) were meant to do and say exactly what the *leader* told us to do and say. If you didn't comply, the consequences were severe and swift, accompanied by cries of *"you're out!"*

> *At a very early age, I learned that the leader was the person out front, showing everyone where they needed to go and what they needed to do.*

3

I continued to receive many messages about leadership during my formative years and later when I entered the workforce. "Leader" and "leadership" were terms used in many different ways and in many contexts, including in sport, politics, at home, community groups, the military and, of course, in organisations.

As a keen new entrant to the workforce, I soon noticed that those in positions of *formal authority* (usually managers who were in charge of other people and resources) were bestowed the title of "leader", usually when they managed the people and resources as expected. These same people were called *excellent* leaders if they were able to co-ordinate and control people and resources *better* than others could.

> *...people were called excellent leaders if they were able to co-ordinate and control people and resources better than others could.*

I remember one executive-level manager, for example, in a government department (where I briefly worked for six months!) who was responsible for many smart professional people – *yet ran the department like a school.* He had devised a myriad of rigid managerial controls and supervisory tasks to make sure "no one stepped out of line". The place was devoid of energy and enthusiasm, yet he was touted as a key leader because he (apparently) managed well, with everyone else following – just as I had also learned and experienced in my primary school days.

There were also heavy expectations on leaders to know more than everyone else, particularly regarding the technical aspects of their job. And *ipso facto*, they were also expected to possess more answers to the problems faced in organisations. Again, managers who seemed to have more answers than others were rewarded, usually by being called a leader. This made perfect sense to me. "Isn't that why leaders are paid more," I thought? Not much has changed today regarding these expectations.

Politics, People and the Pros

My beliefs and views about leadership, similar to just about everybody else's on the planet, continued to be influenced by the people and events around me at the time, as well as from people and events in history.

In politics, Winston Churchill, known mainly for his leadership during World War II and his memorable speeches, was called a great leader by many, despite him being voted out of government as soon as the war was over. [1] In the military, people such as Alexander the Great, known for his tactical ability, his conquests, and for spreading Greek civilisation into the East, were also touted as leaders. Leadership from this perspective was about *taking charge, exercising the full force of one's authority – and winning at all costs.*

Leadership from this perspective was about taking charge, exercising the full force of one's authority — and winning at all costs.

I later learned about and admired Mohandas Karamchand Gandhi (better known as Mahatma Gandhi), the pre-eminent political and spiritual leader of India during the Indian independence movement. Gandhi inspired civil rights movements and freedom across the globe.

Leadership through this lens was about *influencing others to make a positive difference in the world.*

Leadership through this lens was about influencing others to make a positive difference in the world.

Then there were the iconic sporting heroes I idolised as a child (the "pros"). These were the men and women who seemed to achieve amazing athletic feats and were often admired for their leadership qualities. Locally, there was Sir Don Bradman, whose cricketing prowess and gentlemanly character was unsurpassed. In basketball, I loved watching Michael Jordan who seemed to have the ball on a string and knew ahead of time what was going to happen on the court. Within their own sports, they were often called "heroes" and "leaders" by many. Leadership in the sporting arena for me was about *fulfilling one's potential, pushing the limits* of what is thought possible, and, above all, *conquering* the competition and *surpassing one's own self-imposed limits.*

Leadership in the sporting arena... was about fulfilling one's potential, pushing the limits of what is possible, and above all, conquering the competition and surpassing one's own self-imposed limits.

Despite *leader* being used in so many different contexts, I thought I knew what effective leadership meant and what you had to do to be called a *leader*.

Chapter 2

Leadership and the Elite

*We learn more by looking for the answer to a question
and not finding it than we do from learning the
answer itself.*

Lloyd Alexander (b.1924),
American author

Leadership Confusion

As a result of my early experiences I learned that our view of what it means

In my mind at least, I also learned that leadership was largely inaccessible to the masses.

to be a leader is shaped from the time we begin to learn the alphabet. In my mind at least, I also learned that leadership was *largely inaccessible to the masses.* In early adulthood then, I had the mindset that to be a leader you need to *be one of four types of people*:

- a heroic leader on the battlefield.
- someone who holds high public office (or similar).
- an elite sportsperson, or
- a senior person in an organisation.

7

I suspect that many people have learned, perhaps subconsciously, that real leadership is unattainable for them also. Before you dismiss this idea out of hand, I am constantly surprised by how few hands are raised when I ask the following question of a group or team: "How many of you in this room consider yourselves to be leaders?" *You can almost smell the deprecating self-analysis!*

You can almost smell the deprecating self-analysis.

In fact, our beliefs about leadership are shaped by so many different people, sources and contexts that it's almost incomprehensible. Is it any wonder that we are confused – firstly about what leadership actually is, and secondly, *whether I am worthy enough to call myself a leader.*

Over time, however, I came to the realisation that my view of leadership was *overly simplistic.* As is the case with many domains of life, and frustratingly so, the more I learned about leadership, the more I realised *I didn't know.* As a result, I became interested (and subsequently fascinated) in trying to work out what made people "tick". I was particularly interested in leadership and the dynamics that existed within teams, particularly given their *critical nature* to the success of most organisations.

Over time however, I came to the realisation that my view of leadership was overly simplistic.

8

The Seduction of Having the Answers

I pondered many questions. What did real leadership look like? What qualities or attributes were needed to be an *effective* leader? Why were some people called leaders and others not? What was the difference between *managers* and *leaders*? Why were some people successful in life while others with apparently equal talent and motivation were left to languish? Why were some people in organisations able to inspire others and bring out their best while others were loathed?

Perhaps coincidentally, or because of my *fascination in understanding human potential* in the context of leadership, I was called upon more and more to help organisations develop their leadership capability and team performance.

As I moved into different positions and roles in organisations, a theme began to emerge. Others started to look not just for guidance around leadership and team performance, but also expected *the* answers to many of the *big leadership questions* previously posed. The more people asked, the more I felt

> *The more people asked, the more I felt compelled to give them the answers ...*

compelled to give them the answers, so I happily (and naively) provided

> *Paradoxically, the dilemmas I had observed leaders wrestle with...was now happening to me – I just couldn't see it.*

what I thought at the time was the answer. I was seduced by the lure of having to "know it all". Paradoxically, the dilemmas I had observed leaders wrestle with almost daily in having to have *the* answers to a myriad of organisational problems was now happening to me – *I just couldn't see it.*

As I became more entrenched in leadership, team development and culture change programs, I began to reflect on my *deepest beliefs* about leadership and indeed people. Were people just resources to be *managed* and *controlled*? Could sound management *and* effective leadership co-exist within the one person? With its emphasis on *leadership, followership and control*, was our whole management and leadership paradigm *flawed*?

I thought more about Churchill's speeches. While they were clearly of world importance at the time, they seemed a million miles away from my own life

I thought more about Churchill's speeches and while they were clearly of world importance at the time, they seemed a million miles away from my own life...

and reality. I further examined my limited beliefs about who could exercise leadership and under what circumstances. I also began to understand that while managers and leaders *can* be the same, *few* managers actually *led* effectively.

In my view, there was very little correlation between a person's job title and what they actually did. Some of the most junior people I had the privilege of meeting displayed *real leadership*, while people with many more years of experience and had risen to senior positions *often failed to lead effectively*. Many had become *frozen* by their own fears, expending unnecessary energy trying to maintain their status and ego whilst political game-playing.

I remember one "change team" I worked with (in a consulting capacity) in a major financial institution that was collectively responsible for the implementation and integration of major systems worth several *billion dollars*. The team was so *inwardly focused*, that I was amazed they *achieved much at all.* Team members were instead putting a lot of energy and focus on protecting their own "turf", one-upmanship, and destructive side-conversations to undermine each other, therefore ensuring that the status quo was largely maintained. Added to this scenario was the head of the team who insisted on punishing deadlines that had created (or at least contributed to) serious personal problems (with relationships, health, etc) in the team.

We worked with the team over a couple of months and saw almost a "complete turn-around". Experiences like these created an even hotter fire in my belly to understand why some perfectly *rational, intelligent* people act in a perfectly *irrational* and *very unintelligent way* in teams, and why so many people in these situations *fail to lead effectively*.

And so continued my *quest* over twenty years to identify "the answer".

Chapter 3

Theories that Have Driven Leadership Thinking

It is the theory that decides what can be observed.

Albert Einstein (1879-1955),
German-born American Physicist

Leadership Theories

Along the way, I've wrestled with this notion of leadership and if I'm

...I've wrestled with this notion of leadership and if I'm completely honest, I can see my own views and beliefs about leadership morphing over time...

completely honest, I can see my own views and beliefs about leadership morphing over time, almost running in parallel with the leadership trends and theories over decades (albeit in a compressed time frame) as I've tried to get a handle on this thing called "leadership".

While early leadership theories focused on the *qualities* that distinguished leaders from followers, subsequent theories looked at other variables such as *situational factors and skill levels.* [2]

Let's now examine the main theories or paradigms that have shaped many of the programs and development activities in organisations.

"Great Man" theories assume that the capacity for leadership is inherent

13

– *that great leaders are born, not made.* These theories often portray great leaders as *heroic, mythic,* and destined to rise to leadership when needed. Stories about Alexander the Great and Churchill fall into this category. We can also see this paradigm played out almost weekly in the financial and popular press where an all-conquering CEO is featured on the cover.

Trait theories are similar in some ways to Great Man theories, in that they assume that people *inherit certain qualities and traits* that make them better suited to leadership. Trait theories often identify particular personality or behavioural characteristics shared by leaders. I've seen that Great Man theories and trait theories both have shortcomings. For example, when people possess the requisite traits or "stuff" but *fail to lead,* or conversely, where people *have* demonstrated

> *... the belief that effective leaders possess a shopping list of requisite traits holds many people back from stepping into the action of leading.*

leadership, yet may lack many of the "must haves" these theories demand. In my view, the belief that effective leaders have a *shopping list of traits or competencies* can hold people back from stepping into the action of leading, as they recognise a gap between themselves and the "ideal leader".

Contingency theories of leadership focus on particular variables related to the *environment* that might determine which particular style of leadership

> *Unfortunately, many leaders justify destructive, aggressive and toxic behaviours based on the false belief (or rationalisation) that "it was what was needed at the time".*

is best suited to the situation. According to this theory, no leadership style is best in all situations. Unfortunately, many leaders *justify destructive, aggressive and toxic behaviours* based on the *false belief* (or rationalisation) that "it was what was needed at the time".

Situational theories propose that leaders should choose the best course of action based upon the *situation*. Different styles of leadership may be more appropriate for certain types of decision-making. While the premise is sound, I often used to wonder how people achieved this in reality. How do I know what style of leadership is needed for this situation? Or this one, or that one?

Behavioural theories of leadership are based on the belief that *great leaders are made, not born.* People can learn to become leaders through teaching

The dangers observed with this theory...is the ever- increasingly long list of behaviours....that are usually unrealistic...

and observation. The dangers observed with this theory are similar to Great Man and trait theories, in that the ever-increasingly long list of behaviours often espoused as pre-requisites to lead effectively are usually unrealistic and don't take into account human frailties and the different contexts in which leaders operate.

Participative theories of leadership dictate that leaders *take into account the views of others before making decisions.* Again, this is fine if you know where, when and how to do this. I've seen many leaders *ricochet* from being overly-democratic and consultative to authoritative and demanding.

These theories tend to reinforce the archaic notion born in the industrial age that we need to closely manage and control people.

Management theories of leadership (also known as "transactional theories") focus on the role of supervision, organisation and group performance and are largely based on a system of reward and punishment. *These theories tend to reinforce the archaic notion born in the industrial age that we need to closely manage and control people.* The truth is that we need to manage and control things and lead (empower) people. Sadly, the organisational legacy we've all inherited says we *do* need to manage and control people. In general, we *over-manage* and *under-lead* people in today's organisations.

Finally, relationship theories (also known as "transformational theories") *focus on the connections formed between leaders and followers.* In this theory, leaders motivate and inspire people to see the purpose behind the task, as well as wanting each person to fulfil his or her *potential.* Relationship theories stand up well under scrutiny, *providing* leaders know

The team dynamics and "relationship stuff" are often left dormant and unattended until the annual executive retreat at a five-star resort.

how to effectively balance a focus on "relationship" with "task". These two activities go hand-in-glove and should not be approached as being separate, usually evidenced by statements such as, "Let's get the job done first and we'll look after the team dynamics and relationship stuff later." The team dynamics and "relationship stuff" are often left *dormant* and *unattended* until the annual executive retreat at a five-star resort. Wrong!

While all of these theories contribute to the body of knowledge and the practice of leadership, they each are not sufficient on their own and *have created* a lot of *confusion* in people's minds about how to proceed either in developing leadership capability or in what it means to *lead.* The Big Secret about Leadership

So after a twenty year quest, what is the "big secret" I've discovered about leadership? Well...the big secret is that there is *no big secret.* Despite what hundreds, if not thousands, of management books, articles and so-called experts will tell you, there *are no silver bullets.* You probably already knew that there is no *one* answer, simply based on the title of this book, right? Or

16

perhaps your own experience has led you to this conclusion already. You, like others reading this book, will have your own views on leadership.

So, perhaps you are reading this book in the hope that there are some relatively simple ways to think about and practice leadership that are effective and within reach of just about everybody? Well, the good news is that there are.

There is no doubting that leadership can be a demanding activity. I am not trying to trivialise the challenges of leadership because those challenges are very real.

In my mind then, *real* leadership means:
- taking courageous action.
- treading where others fear to tread.
- challenging the status quo.
- naming the elephants in the room.
- confronting poor behaviour or performance.
- creating an environment of trust and respect for one another.
- ensuring that solutions are well thought out and systemic where appropriate.

There are a number of relatively simple things *anyone* can do to be a more effective leader — whether you are a CEO, divisional head, a manager of people, technical specialist, new manager or a community leader.

There are a number of relatively simple things anyone can do to be a more effective leader...

Effective leadership ought *not* be confined to particular roles or industries either. Effective leadership is effective leadership, no matter where it occurs.

The discussion that follows in Part 2 outlines why I think *most leaders don't lead*. Then, in Part 3, I discuss the "case for leadership" and why we need to *lift our sights on the quality of leadership, both in organisations and society* in the "Leadership Declaration – Our Vision for the Future". Part 4 brings to life our Leadership Declaration through a "rolling case study" and real life examples that you may be able to relate to in The Seven Spheres of Leadership Mastery.

Part Two:

Why Most Leaders Don't Lead

Chapter 4

The Industrial Age Leadership Paradigm

All our knowledge has its origins in our perceptions.

Leonardo da Vinci *(1452-1519),*
Italian draftsman, painter, sculptor, architect and engineer

The Dominant Paradigm

We are currently locked in a dominant paradigm founded in the industrial age where organisations were thought of as machines and people thought of as things to be controlled. People were necessary but replaceable. This paradigm, while useful for the production of goods in a low or no-technology environment, is *woefully inadequate* for the 21st century.

> *This (industrial age) paradigm, while useful for the production of goods in a low or no-technology environment, is woefully inadequate for the 21st century.*

According to Stephen Covey, [3] many of our modern management practices come from the industrial age. These include:

- the *belief* that you *control and manage* people.
- the view of accounting that makes people an *expense* and machines *assets* (think about it...) .
- *a carrot and stick motivational philosophy* (rewards versus fear and punishment) .

21

- *centralised budgeting* where hierarchies and bureaucracies are formed to drive "getting the numbers" – an obsolete reactive process.

The management of people as things by those in authoritative positions prevents them from tapping into the highest motivations, talents and potential of people. At what cost?

Mark Hower from Antioch University writes:

> *Industrialisation surely provided a rationale and means to thoroughly mould and constrain our thinking about leadership for generations…"* [4]

Author John Gardner once said, "Most ailing organisations have developed a functional blindness to their own defects." One of the most fascinating

Most ailing organisations have developed a functional blindness to their own defects.

dissertations on leadership and the industrial age is by Joseph Rost, who wrote *Leadership for the 21st Century.*[5] According to Rost, the industrial age paradigm of leadership is characterised by (among other things):

- a *personalistic focus* since only great leaders do leadership.
- a promotion of an *individualistic* and even a *self-interested* outlook on life.
- an acceptance of a male model of behaviour and power (which has been labelled a leadership style).

Leadership and the 100-Year-Old Paradigm

Rost [6] was intrigued with the idea that there *must be a unifying theme or a holistic framework* that made sense of 80-90 years of research and writing on the subject of leadership (all during the 20th century – it seems that people in the 19th century and earlier didn't care quite as much as we do about leadership!). *The single paradigm he managed to find was the industrial paradigm* – a distinctly *individualistic* framework.

The second thing he discovered was that the *basic ideas of leadership haven't changed much in one hundred years*. The same ideas have been recycled decade after decade in the mainstream literature and have not impacted on the accumulated wisdom of leadership.

> *...the basic ideas of leadership haven't changed much in one hundred years. The same ideas have been recycled decade after decade...*

Leaders and Followers

Another finding by Rost was that it is part of our belief system about leadership that the individual person, the leader, is the one who *does* the process – leadership – to others. This conclusion translates into the practice of thinking and acting as if the *followers don't have anything to do with leadership*. In fact, we have created a new word in the industrial paradigm to explain what followers do – they do *followership*. And the essence of being a follower is to be *passive, submissive, subordinate, controlled, and directed.*

> *And the essence of being a follower – of followership – is to be passive, submissive, subordinate, controlled, and directed.*

23

Dee Hock, founder and CEO emeritus of both Visa USA and Visa International, and author of *Birth of the Chaordic Age* [7] believes that anyone who is *coerced* to the purposes, objectives, or preferences of another is not a follower in any true sense of the word, but an *object of manipulation*.

Examples of the leader-follower belief system are rife in organisations today. Much of the frustration expressed to me when coaching CEOs and executives is that they just can't seem to get people to "comply" or do what he thinks should be done. In this scenario, many then externalise the problem by saying that *they* have motivation issues or lack the skills to do the job.

One executive I worked with recently had the belief that because he was the "leader", others needed to just implement *his* plan to be successful. His style was aggressive, individualistic and highly ego-driven. He was right to some extent because his area *did* deliver results, but *the costs were high.* Many of his senior leaders hated working there, and some had started to leave. He was also having difficulty attracting talent into the business unit.

When I scratched the surface (by holding a big mirror up), he confessed that he *also* did not want to live or lead like this anymore. After a six-month coaching program, his beliefs about himself and people had been transformed considerably, and his way of managing and leading had indeed shifted significantly for the better. He moved to practising "shared leadership" and was reaping some of the early benefits.

After years of researching leadership, which included 221 definitions of leadership in over 500 books and articles, Rost was led "to the ultimate synthesis of the leadership literature", and managed to boil it down to *two words*: the leadership literature for the entire 20th century has framed leadership as "good management". Hence there is no such thing as bad leadership because when leadership is bad it is characterised as just "plain management". *Good* means *effective*, or management that is above average or goes beyond expectations or promotes excellence. [5]

The leadership literature has *denigrated management* throughout the 20th century, so leadership authors have insisted that we must understand leadership as *better than management*, as the *right stuff of management*, almost like we don't need good management any more.

> *The leadership literature has denigrated management throughout the 20th century...*

Nothing could be further from the truth. So almost without exception, the sole leader is touted as the person who "does leadership" by creating a vision, taking charge and motivating others to follow. The current paradigm has created a *leadership vacuum*, where managers try to come up with the answers for everyone else to go away and implement. The "I think, you do" phenomenon is alive and well.

Chapter 5

The Age of Passivity

The smart way to keep people passive and obedient is to strictly limit the spectrum of acceptable opinion, but allow very lively debate within that spectrum.

Noam Chomsky *(b. 1928),*
American linguist, philosopher, cognitive scientist, political activist, author, and lecturer

That's Not My Job

With the backdrop of global and organisational challenges in front of us, the role of organisations and their leaders in society is even *more critical than ever*. This is at a time when leaders are under more intense scrutiny than perhaps ever in history.

We are stuck, however, in what I call the "Age of Passivity". As discussed earlier, we are taught very early in life to "follow the leader" and our desire to look to others to solve problems for us is all pervasive rather than to act powerfully within our spheres of influence. The Age of Passivity is symbolised by examples such as:

The Age of Passivity is symbolised by...people blaming others when things go wrong, not taking responsibility...

- people blaming others when things go wrong.
- not taking responsibility.
- not being accountable for results.
- waiting for others to act before acting.
- not making timely and effective decisions.
- only acting in the interests of oneself or one's own team or silo.

In general, we also rely on others too heavily to solve our problems for us, whether they are the global issues we discussed earlier, or those that confront us on a daily basis in organisations. For example, I recently walked into a reception area to see a health professional. The woman on the desk was well-groomed, middle-aged, appeared to be well educated, and was courteous and helpful. While talking, I couldn't help but notice the flickering light above us and said to the woman, "That must really be irritating!"

"Yes", she replied, "it's been that way for weeks...But it's not *my* job to change it or get it fixed, so I guess it *stays* like that." Her reply surprised me...and it didn't – all at the same time.

Her reply surprised me – and it didn't – all at the same time.

Inflexibility and the "it's not my job" phenomenon permeates organisations. The problem is that we become *blind, numb or both* to it so we fail to see it for what it is and take action accordingly. It happens with flickering lights, it happens

The problem is that we become blind, numb or both to it so fail to see it for what it is and take action accordingly.

in teams, and it happens across functions and divisions. If we tune in to it, we can see generous amounts of blame, denial, justification and a lack of accountability occurring every day of the week. Outcomes include cost blowouts, missed deadlines, frustrated and disengaged employees, and a negative impact on customer service. *In essence, performance is severely impacted.*

The 'Fix It' Mentality

So in the Age of Passivity, we tend to rely too heavily on others, particularly those in *positions of authority* or *government* to "fix" things or to act first. Charles Handy, the futurist, wrote, "We can't rely on governments to lead us. In democracies, governments have to go with the grain of public opinion or they won't get re-elected. [8] How many metaphorical flickering lights and receptionists do you have in your organisation? And more importantly, how much is it costing you?

The fact is that when it comes to solving our toughest challenges, no government, statutory body, CEO or any other individual can solve these problems *in isolation*, despite our apparent worship of the heroic CEO who will "save" the organisation.

> *I always thought someone should do something...until I realised I was someone.*
> John F Kennedy

What's the problem with leaders providing solutions? When we over-rely on others for the answers, we *contribute to a culture of passivity*. This statement does not discount the role of those with technical expertise because it is often appropriate, perhaps even necessary, to look to those with authoritative expertise to provide advice and counsel. But problems may occur in that scenario as well.

Let me give you an example to demonstrate the point. Let's assume "John" attends his family doctor with a suspected heart condition. John doesn't expect his doctor to say, "Work it out for yourself!" In this situation, we expect to be *given* the answer and this is appropriate when the problem is a clear-cut technical problem with a clear-cut, known, tried-and-tested solution. In effect, we vest authority in the doctor in exchange for a service. For argument sake, let's say that after consulting his doctor and being referred to a specialist, John needs a by-pass operation.

The surgeon performs the operation but John fails to make any lifestyle changes. In ten years or so his heart needs another overhaul. This is an act of passivity and a lack of responsibility – both from the patient *and* the surgeon. Both have failed to address the underlying issues of poor eating habits and a sedentary lifestyle. John has effectively deferred responsibility and accountability for managing his own health without addressing the root causes.

This isn't particularly new or breakthrough thinking – we all know the old adage *prevention is better than cure* or advice to avoid *band-aid approaches*, but we still fail to act appropriately. We know in real life, for example, that about *90 percent of patients do not change their lifestyle after receiving a life-saving by-pass operation.* [9] The fact remains that if organisations want to outperform the competition, become "employers of choice", attract and retain the best and brightest, then a constructive, values-based culture *must be fostered through planned and methodical change.*

> *We know in real life for example that about 90 percent of patients do not change their lifestyle after receiving a life-saving by-pass operation.*

Added to the toxic effects of passivity are the difficulties faced by managers when trying to solve tough challenges in today's world. Members of organisations at all levels often provide what has been called "counterfeit leadership", [10] which is our topic for discussion in the next chapter.

30

Chapter 6

Counterfeit Leadership

The first man to see an illusion by which men have
flourished for centuries surely stands in a lonely place.

Gary Zukav,
American author

Technical Versus Adaptive

The sad fact is that in organisations, valuable resources are squandered
by managers and leaders who *apply quick fixes* (here's your pill) that don't
work, or alternatively, *misdiagnose* the problem and so apply the *wrong*
fix altogether. This is what has been called *counterfeit leadership* by Dean
Williams, [10] where the leader:

- places an excessive emphasis on *getting people to follow*.
- is pre-occupied with *dominance* as a control mechanism.
- *fails to fully engage the group* and its many sub-groups.
- is unwilling to look for solutions *beyond their own comfort zone* or
  the *prevailing group paradigm*.
- believes they *alone* have the *truth* and know the way forward.

Managers and leaders don't necessarily do this on purpose or consciously,
but one of the most common ways leaders provide counterfeit

31

leadership is by applying a *technical solution* to an *adaptive challenge*.
So what's the difference?

A technical problem has a known solution that can be implemented with

Progress lies beyond *current know how.* It can be resolved through
authoritative expertise to the application of authoritative expertise
mobilise discovery and to supported by the organisation's processes,
shed old ways of looking policies and structures. [11] Adaptive challenges,
at the problem. on the other hand, can only be addressed

through changes in people's priorities, values, beliefs, habits or loyalties.
Progress lies beyond authoritative expertise to mobilise discovery and to
shed old ways of looking at the problem.

Table 6.1 outlines and summarises some of the ways that counterfeit
leadership is applied in organisations and what real leadership looks like.

Table 6.1

Situation/Example	Counterfeit Leadership	Real Leadership
Dysfunctional behaviour exhibited by a senior member of the organisation	People ignore it, manage around it, or talk about it behind the person's back	Confront the behaviour directly with the person in a constructive and empathetic way
Underperforming business unit due to a culture of paternalism and nepotism	Merge the BU with another; provide technical training, re-structure the management team	Identify the root causal factors and address them; provide retraining; make hard calls about BU heads
Manager who gets short-term results but destroys value in the company and his people in the long-term	Reward the manager for delivering against company (six-monthly) short-term objectives	Provide coaching; performance management; remove if unable or unwilling to adapt and change

Table 6.1 Continued

Situation/Example	Counterfeit Leadership	Real Leadership
You attend meetings for your leadership team, where the tough issues are not discussed	You collude with the system by not raising these issues in the meetings	You raise issues in a constructive and assertive manner; ask the challenging questions
Your team or peers are not quite up to the job; not everyone is pulling their weight; people are afraid to try things in case they make a mistake	Jumping in and getting things done; not delegating appropriately; telling your team or peers what and how they should do things	Ensure people's motivation and capability meet the demands of the role through formal training, on-the-job upskilling, letting people experiment and learn more

So in summary, the real leader will:

- get people to *face reality* as it relates to their condition, threats and opportunities.
- mobilise the group to do adaptive work and adjust their values, habits, practices and priorities.
- pursue the needed *insight and wisdom to lead.*
- take responsibility for being the source of the movement.

Williams [10] also summarises what real leadership is not about: it's not about:

- *dominance or control.*
- putting a *false* set of tasks before people and getting them to follow.

- getting one's own way and trying to get people to buy into something they are not ready to embrace, even if born of strong convictions and moral beliefs.
- *staying in your comfort zone* and doggedly holding onto the world you know, even as the "ship is sinking".

Logical But Ineffective

So, while many leaders provide real leadership, many do not. I can use my own experience as a case-in-point. I remember a time in my own life where I presided over a team that had very poor relationships with a support area. We needed them more than they needed us. Despite my efforts to resolve the problem, I largely failed.

Despite my efforts to resolve the problem, I largely failed. With hindsight and the passing of time, I can see that I contributed and perhaps even fed the problem.

With hindsight and the passing of time, I can see that I contributed and perhaps even fed the problem. How? I took on the (traditional) management responsibility of doing "the work" on behalf of the team. "The work" was mostly logical at the time – I had numerous conversations with the head of the support team, put in place processes and guidelines (an ineffective technical fix) and tried to build trust.

All to no avail. What would have been a more constructive response? Think for a moment about what you would have done.

What I think I could have done differently was to create an environment

34

where my own team and the support team were given responsibility to build relationships *themselves,* by creating more open and honest forums,

I was too personally immersed within the system and the expectations of my role seemed to push me in that direction.

as well as encouraging my team to take more positive action to demonstrate our commitment to making it work, ensuring that *all* the elephants (or what I like to call the 'undiscussibles') were on the table.

Although I help teams resolve these types of issues successfully all the time, I was too personally immersed within the system and the expectations of my role seemed to push me in that direction. In the next chapter I will discuss *why* I suspect we all provide counterfeit leadership from time-to-time, just as I did.

35

Chapter 7

The Delusion of Solutions

The biggest mistake that leaders can make is to give people false hope that melts like snow.

Winston Churchill (1874 – 1965),
British politician

False Promises, False Hope

In this chapter, rather than talk about counterfeit leadership broadly, I will focus primarily on the propensity of leaders to provide technical solutions to challenges that need an adaptive response (also counterfeit leadership). My thinking has been drawn from both Williams [10] and the pioneering work of Heifetz, Grashow and Linsky. [11]

The first reason leaders apply false (technical) solutions to adaptive challenges is that *leaders who solve problems are rewarded by the organisation.*

Many have built their reputations on their ability to (apparently) solve problems over the long-term.

After all, most managers and leaders have been successful in the past by following this familiar pattern of solving problems quickly. In fact, many people in formal authority positions take great pride at labels like 'troubleshooter' or 'Mr Fixit'.

Many have *built their reputations* on their ability to (apparently) solve problems over the long-term. Those who provide solutions really well are

37

rewarded through short and long-term incentives, not to mention being bestowed with the ultimate honour – being called a *leader*.

In my own team (discussed in the previous chapter), I believe team members, in a well-intentioned way, would *praise, reward and reinforce my behaviour* – often by saying what strong leadership I had displayed. This was, of course, very seductive. Who doesn't want to be called a leader? So I would *repeat* the types of behaviour that would let others *off the hook* by not having to confront the issues fully themselves.

Related to the above discussion, the second reason leaders often apply false (technical) solutions to adaptive challenges is that *it is much harder to confront the real, underlying issues than it is to apply a simplistic, known approach*. It is much simpler to have a safe conversation about a superficial issue – which people collude and delude themselves into thinking is the *real* issue – than it is to confront the elephant in the room, team or organisation. When was the last time someone thanked you for pointing out a *gap* between their espoused values and those they actually demonstrate? It's not that likely.

The third reason leaders often apply false (technical) solutions to adaptive challenges is that *it keeps the temperature at lower levels and people around them can stay in their comfort zones*. The principles of adaptive leadership dictate that people and systems will act to maintain the status quo, and so will often avoid the real issue, conversation or decision that needs to be made. This is frankly how individuals, teams and whole organisations can stay "stuck" by failing to address the real issues and challenges that reside within. It is therefore easier to avoid addressing the real problems that are affecting performance. People engage in very creative ways to avoid the prospect of change and the tension that comes with it. Leaders need to receive training on how to spot and then manage creative avoidance whilst, of course, not falling into the same trap by avoiding the work themselves.

Work avoidance strategies (adapted from Williams [10]) include:

- *blame, denial and shifting responsibility (scapegoating)* – examples include departments or divisions blaming the other one for delays.
- *forming committees or working parties* – to analyse the problem *ad nauseam*, effectively delaying action. Alternatively, those in authority fail to divest any meaningful authority to the committee or working party, rendering it impotent (a favourite of governments where they are seen to be doing something but they're not really!) or delegate it to an outside party who *can't do anything about it.*
- *personal attack or 'assassination'* – discredit the person trying to bring about change, move them on, take away the resources they need to continue, or in the worst case, literally "take them out" metaphorically. This could mean sacking them under the guise of incompetence or, in politics, actually *assassinating* the person because of the change or cause they represented. There are many strategies leaders can be taught to help prevent this.
- *focusing on the easier parts of the problem* that don't cause discomfort or too much stress. An example would be where a new technology

solution is applied to lift customer service levels, while the real issue of poor quality management remains unaddressed.

- *changing the scope of the project or work to fit the current expertise or skills* – projects or teams can retrofit the scope or breadth or work to fit with their current levels of comfort or mindset.

The fourth reason that leaders often apply false (technical) solutions to adaptive challenges is that it keeps *our own levels of discomfort within tolerable levels.* I haven't met many people who enjoy "confronting"

I haven't met many people who enjoy "confronting" reality, speaking the truth at great personal risk to themselves...

reality, speaking the truth at great personal risk to themselves, or drawing attention to issues that are extremely sensitive – issues that people talk about at the water cooler but *dare* not mention in public. They require the creation of high levels of *psychological safety* if they are to be drawn out effectively.

The fifth and final reason why we apply false (technical) solutions to adaptive challenges is *that in order to lead adaptively, we actually have to dance on the edge of our authority.* The people who hired you or asked you to work on the project have certain expectations which define the boundaries of your formal and informal authority. Organisations reward people for *staying* right in the middle of their "circle of authority". It is only when we start to *push* those

Organisations reward people for staying right in the middle of their "circle of authority".

boundaries, challenge in areas where it is not necessarily welcomed, that we begin to truly *lead* adaptively. You won't be rewarded for pushing the boundaries or expanding your informal and formal circles of authority, but this is *exactly what is needed*.

Dean Williams says, "To lead is to live dangerously." [10] Real leadership requires courage, tenacity and a clear sense of oneself and what needs to change. While there are many languages and cultures that

To lead is to live dangerously.

have an interpretation for the actual word "leadership", I have a favourite. The Indo-European root of the word "leadership" is *leith*, which means "to go forth", "to cross a threshold", or "to die". [12]

When going into battle, the solider carrying the flag at the front of the battalion was called the leader and he often was killed first, thereby warning the rest of the troops. I'm not suggesting you die on the sword for the cause. This isn't a very smart way to operate because then you're not around to continue the fight. What I am suggesting is that we need to let go of some of our fears. Once we overcome or work through the fear of stepping

Once we overcome or work through the fear of stepping into the unknown we are at the very heart and essence of leadership.

into the unknown we are at the very heart and essence of leadership.

Part Three:

A Leadership Declaration – Our Vision for the Future

Chapter 8

A Leadership Declaration – Our Vision for the Future of Leadership

It takes a lot of courage to release the familiar and seemingly secure, to embrace the new. But there is no real security in what is no longer meaningful. There is more security in the adventurous and exciting, for in movement there is life, and in change there is power.

Alan Cohen, Author

Aim

My aim in writing this Leadership Declaration is to inspire and ignite leadership action that makes a difference for you, your organisation and the world we live in.

My aim in writing this Leadership Declaration is to inspire and ignite leadership action that makes a difference for you, your organisation and the world we live in.

My intention in writing a Leadership Declaration is to clearly state the case for leadership and its importance to all of us at this time. At an organisational level, there is little doubt that real leadership is the "engine room" of performance. In the absence of systemic, results-focused leadership, *breakthrough performance and high commitment will not be achieved.*

45

Why the World Needs Leaders Like You

The world needs leaders perhaps more than any time in history. We are just starting to emerge from one of the worst economic crises ever seen – the Global Financial Crisis or 'GFC' – arguably a failure of leadership at the individual, government and organisational levels. Perhaps not surprisingly, trust in institutions is running on empty while the bar has been raised on what we expect of our leaders.

For example, in an annual measure of trust, the Edelman Trust Barometer (2009), where 4,475 opinion-leaders in twenty countries were interviewed, nearly two in three people said they trusted corporations *less* now than they did a year ago. [13] Conventional wisdom suggests, and the data confirms, that trust affects consumer spending, corporate reputation and a company's ability to navigate the regulatory environment.

Also, according to the United Nations,[14] the defining characteristic of today's world is change. In almost every sector, the pace of change is unprecedented in recent history. Technological change, especially in information and communications technology, affects virtually all aspects of our lives. Internationalisation and rapid economic growth in many societies has altered traditional socio-economic structures. Exacerbating the challenge of economic development is the issue of climate change, the sustainable use of resources and the maintenance of key ecological systems.

In almost every sector, the pace of change is unprecedented in recent history.

At the time of writing, the United Nations has just hosted the Climate Change Summit in Copenhagen (December 2009). Whilst some are disappointed with the results, it did introduce the Copenhagen Accord and a new kind of dynamic in global climate policy – which some are saying is a *new world climate order*. Only real leadership being demonstrated by nations around the world will ensure a positive impact is felt in the future.

Despite our affluence in many parts of the world, there were estimated to be *1.4 billion people in the developing world (one in four) living on less than US$1.25 a day* in 2005, down from 1.9 billion (one in two) in 1981. [15]

Despite our affluence… there were estimated to be 1.4 billion people in the developing world (one in four) living on less than US$1.25 a day…

Justin Lin, Chief Economist of the World Bank and Senior Vice President, Development Economics said, "However, the sobering news – that poverty is more pervasive than we thought – means that we must redouble our efforts, especially in Sub-Saharan Africa."

More than a billion people – almost one-fifth of the world's population – lack access to safe drinking water and 40 percent lack access to basic sanitation. [15] The global issues we face will require unprecedented leadership and unprecedented levels of co-operation concurrently, to mobilise communities and organisations.

A New Paradigm for the Future

To make progress on our most significant issues, I believe that we need a *new paradigm* – one that *inspires* us to:

- act *constructively* in a *values-driven* way.
- *empower* each other to take responsibility and accountability at all levels of the organisation.
- shift our focus from *problem-centric* to *solution-centric* (positive change).
- make *progress* on the toughest issues and challenges.
- create an environment of *breakthrough performance*, high levels of commitment and learning.
- *liberate ourselves* from old ways of thinking about how to manage and lead people, and
- develop *systems intelligence.*

As the industrial age wanes, new possibilities emerge for us to create a different paradigm of leadership. The new paradigm I am proposing draws from many sources and builds on them in an integrative way. However, one doesn't change a paradigm by writing a book. The mechanistic, industrial paradigm has been in existence since the latter part of the 18th century and continues to shape society and modern organisations. It is a long, slow journey, yet *incredibly worthwhile.*

As the industrial age wanes, new possibilities emerge for us to create a different paradigm of leadership.

This is not a paradigm I claim to be inventing, but rather a paradigm that is emerging slowly after almost a 100-year stalemate. *The essence of what I am proposing, however, has driven and continues to drive me and my colleagues to do this type of work.* We are striving to create organisations that are more humanistic, where behaviour is values-driven and where each and every person's potential and contribution can be optimised in service of the organisational mission, which in turn, should make a positive contribution to the world.

We are interested in developing leaders from many different industries, fields and walks of life. We have had the privilege over many years to come into contact with some wonderful leaders – the men and women who are able to continually meet or exceed performance expectations while having the wonderful ability to draw forth the great potential of those around them.

We are interested in developing leaders from many different industries, fields and walks of life.

It also should be pointed out that I am not trying to provide *the definitive answer* on what leadership is and is not – people have been trying to do that for over 100 years. The words of Margaret Thatcher resonate when she said:

To me, consensus seems to be the process of abandoning all beliefs, principles, values and policies. So it is something in which no one believes and to which no one objects. [16]

My intention is to build a case for *a new way of leading* that incorporates a number of principles and leading schools of thought. Having begun the declaration with a call for leaders to stand up and make a difference in the context of global challenges, the focus will now be firmly grounded in the organisational context, starting broadly and then becoming more focused on tangible and practical steps that can be taken to lead more effectively or develop leaders to ensure the best chance of success.

During the exploration, there will be opportunities to reflect and

I am optimistic that you will apply many of the ideas in this book to your own organisation, as well other aspects of your life...

contextualise the discussion for your own situation. I am optimistic that you will apply many of the ideas in this book to your own organisation, as well other aspects of your life, whether it be as a parent, junior sports coach, or community leader.

Leadership and The Three Pillars of Performance

It would be remiss of me to discuss leadership development in this book without putting it in a broader context. The model we have adapted and use to guide our work with clients is a relatively simple one from Michael Beer. [17]

Organisations that are able to deliver sustained performance have developed the three pillars of:

- performance alignment.
- psychological alignment.
- capacity for learning and change.

Performance alignment occurs when the total organisational system, including systems, structures, people and culture fits performance goals and strategy. *Psychological alignment* is the emotional attachment people have at all levels, particularly key business unit leaders to the purpose, mission and values of the organisation *("I just love working here"* is heard a lot).

50

If the organisation is to sustain both performance and psychological alignment, it must also have the *capacity for learning and change.* [17]

The three pillars provide organisational resilience to rapid change and uncertainty and those organisations that are strong in all three markedly increase their chances of *sustaining high performance* and *high commitment,* sometimes over decades. Southwest Airlines is cited as a company that has been able to maintain high performance and high commitment over a period of four decades. While competitors were able to copy some aspects of the three pillars, they were never able to achieve psychological alignment or the capacity to learn and change.

The three pillars provide organisational resilience to rapid change and uncertainty and those organisations that are strong in all three markedly increase their chances of sustaining high performance and high commitment...

In terms of the *capacity for learning and change,* "The only enduring source of competitive advantage is an organisation's relative ability to learn faster than its competition," wrote Arie de Geus, former head of planning at Shell. [18] For de Geus, learning was "the process whereby an organisation evolved to remain in harmony with a changing environment", and was key to success. We are facing unprecedented change and learning challenges that require agility and a new kind of systems awareness and adaptability.

In terms of *psychological alignment,* relationships and teamwork become central drivers of behaviour, with people sacrificing their immediate self-interest for the demanding goals required of high performance. In effect, organisations seeking *psychological alignment* consciously develop a "psychological contract" — a high investment, high return exchange between the firm and its employees. [17]

Leading "With", Not Leading "Over"

The discussion about relationships and teams being central drivers for high performance organisations flows nicely into the idea that leadership is about "leading with" rather than "leading over" and has been explored previously by people such as Burns,[19] Hollander [20] and Rost. [5]

Again, drawing from Rost as a building block, leadership is viewed as not something that is *done to others*, but rather as a *relationship*. Of course,

...leadership is viewed as not something that is done to others, but rather as a relationship.

the word *follower* becomes a problem if we dispense with the traditional notion of leader/ follower. While Rost settled on calling followers "collaborators", I will simply refer to them as "team". While perhaps not precise in terms of what a team really is, I find it less clumsy than other terms.

Rost's definition of leadership then becomes *an influence relationship among leaders and team members who intend real changes that reflect their mutual purposes.*[4] This definition of leadership includes four essential elements:

1. *The leader-team relationship is based on influence and is multidirectional.* It is non-coercive because the relationship would

52

turn into an authority, power, or dictatorial relationship if coercive behaviours were used to gain compliance.

2. *Leaders and team members are the people in this relationship.* If leadership is what the relationship is, then both team members and formal leaders are all 'doing leadership'. All leadership relationships need not look (or be) the same.

3. *Leaders and team members intend real changes.* The word "intend" means that the changes the leaders and team members promote are purposeful, that the changes didn't happen by chance or accident. Change should be substantive, significant or transforming.

4. *The leader and team members' intended changes reflect their mutual purposes.* The changes must not only reflect what the leaders want but what team members also want.

Rost's definition clearly distinguishes leadership from management, not only because of the people who are possible leaders (thus, managers are not automatically leaders and non-managers can be leaders), but in the three other essential elements required for leadership: *influence, intended real change,* and *mutual purposes.* None of those three elements are essential to management.

To make the distinction clearer, Table 8.1 describes some contrasts between leadership and management.

53

Table 8.1

Management	Leadership
Authority relationship	Influence relationship
Done by managers and subordinates	Done by leaders and team members
Involves coordinating people and resources to produce and sell goods and/or services in an organisation	Involves leaders and team members intending real changes in an organisation
Coordinated activities reflect the organisation's purpose	Reflects mutual purposes
Requires a position/role to operate from	Anyone can lead from anywhere in the organisation

The intention here is not to denigrate management but to distinguish it from leadership. Management plays a vital function in all organisations and societies. We need both management and leadership in organisations and societies to survive and prosper.

The intention here is not to denigrate management but to distinguish it from leadership.

Adaptive Leadership

Adaptive leadership, pioneered by Ron Heifetz and Marty Linsky over a period of 30 years at Harvard University's John F. Kennedy School of Government, characterises leadership as something that is "exercised" [21] and complements the principles outlined by Joseph Rost. It is therefore much easier to discuss leadership as an action, and not a position. Those who lead in this sense also don't need to rely on the constraints of formal authority or positional power.

Heifetz [22] believes that we have confused authority with leadership for too long. It's actually a contradiction in terms to say, "the leadership isn't exercising any leadership." What we should say is, "People in authority aren't exercising any leadership." There are many people who are skilled at gaining formal and informal authority, but *never* lead. [22] If leadership differs from the capacity to gain authority and therefore a "following", what anchors us in leadership?

There are many people who are skilled at gaining formal and informal authority, but never lead.

Leadership takes place in the context of problems and challenges. Leadership becomes necessary, not when things are going well, but when there are difficult challenges that need to be tackled. It's when operating according to current structures, procedures and processes no longer suffice – *a new way must be forged.* [22]

In their excellent new book, *The Practice of Adaptive Leadership – Tools and Tactics for Changing Your Organisation and the World,* [11] Heifetz , Grashow and Linsky define leadership in this way:

Adaptive leadership is the practice of mobilizing people to tackle tough challenges and thrive.

The elements that particularly resonate are:
- *practice* – as discussed, leadership is not a role or position, it is an *action*. The word practice indicates an ongoing activity.
- *mobilising* – this is at the heart of adaptive leadership – mobilising

people to take responsibility and action locally. It speaks to many of the problems discussed with the industrial paradigm of leadership.

- *people* – people are the only ones who can innovate to help the organisation become more productive and meet its strategy.

- *tough challenges* – there are many problems and challenges in organisations, many of which can be solved through the application of normal management practices and systems. Tough challenges indicate those that require a different approach and will promote breakthrough performance.

- *thrive* – just as with biological systems, organisational systems and human systems need to adapt and become stronger to meet future challenges. This is more than just *survival*.

Adaptive leadership demands learning – where values, beliefs and priorities need to change in order to make progress. It is where the application of technical solutions will not fix the problem and requires a response outside the current repertoire. With adaptive challenges, the people with the problem are the problem, and they are the solution. Adaptive work often requires more of an experimental approach so the time frames are often longer.

In our earlier example with the doctor, if he or she was to show *adaptive* or *real leadership*, what might they do? Imagine a cardiac surgeon, for example, telling patients that he will refuse to do the operation unless patients do their part of the work – quit smoking, exercise,

We let people off the hook in organisations constantly.

adopt a healthy diet. Also, to ensure compliance, the surgeon insists the patient place 50 percent of all their assets in to a holding account for six months pending their *successful change*. It is likely most will find another surgeon who will do the operation and let them off the hook. [11] *We let people off the hook in organisations constantly.*

Our surgeon was demonstrating adaptive leadership by getting his patient to take responsibility for making healthy lifestyle changes rather than simply expecting the operation would fix all his woes. Without the deeper level change, the patient will be back for another operation in the future, or worse. Could your organisation benefit from people taking full responsibility and accountability for their own problems rather than deferring upwards? I haven't found an organisation yet where this aspect doesn't need work. We're often so used to dealing with each other in ways that are less than 100 percent accountable that we sometimes forget what it actually feels like when people are 100 percent accountable. It's refreshing *and* it greases the wheels of business almost like nothing else.

Leaders who get the most attention in the media are those who act like leadership *is all about them*. You'd think that the sheep were only there for the benefit of the shepherd. [22] Leadership therefore also becomes participatory, involving many perspectives and stakeholders because no one person has enough knowledge to either adequately identify the challenge or know the solution. [4] It's useful to point out that traditional roles and functions are not lost in this way of operating. In fact, Burns argues that it enhances leadership because

You'd think that the sheep were only there for the benefit of the shepherd.

Leadership electrifies the system as followers become leaders and vice versa.

57

"leadership electrifies the system as followers become leaders and vice versa". [19]

Thus leadership in a post-industrial context requires less control and hierarchy, which are consistent with the machine metaphor, *instead opening up the possibility that the actions we take in life and organisations can be shared, co-created and constructed.* [4] In this new realm of leadership, the best leadership does not generate followers – *it generates other leaders.* It generates people who are willing to take responsibility. [17] And in order to do this, one of the key tasks of leadership is to create an environment of high psychological safety where everyone in the team and organisation feels safe to challenge, speak out and constructively confront anyone else in the organisation – anyone. One organisation, where I had been consulting for some time, had a constructive culture. I saw a female graduate of about 23 years of age challenge the CEO on which values the organisation should choose, and she succeeded in changing the CEO's mind. Leadership gold.

> *...the actions we take in life and organisations can be shared, co-created and constructed.*

A New Leadership Paradigm

If we integrate the thinking and principles of Rost (leadership is a relationship) [5]; Beer (Three Pillars of Performance) [17]; and Heifetz and Laurie (adaptive leadership) [23], we can see a great deal of commonality and power. *The essential elements of leadership become:*

1. Leadership is about the *relationship.*
2. *Anyone can lead* from anywhere in the organisation.
3. Leadership is about *influencing* and *mobilising* people.

4. The action of leadership involves *real change* to make progress on tough challenges to serve a mutual purpose.

Table 8.2 summarises a new paradigm of leadership and contrasts it with the current one.

Table 8.2

Current Paradigm	New Paradigm
Leaders are smarter than everyone else	Everyone can contribute in a meaningful way
Leaders have the answers	The answer resides in the collective, not individuals
Leaders are active while followers are passive	All employees are engaged and contributing
Leaders need to motivate their charges	People are self-motivated if given the opportunities
Followers need to be given direction to be productive	Employees can be very productive if the right environment exists
Leadership can be elitist and special	Leadership is a relationship
Leadership is individualistic	Leadership is shared
Vertical leadership – top-down philosophy, where the leader is decisive, efficient, unemotional and in-control	Horizontal leadership – collaborative, power-sharing facilitation and empowerment
Objective, single, mechanical, hierarchical and controllable	The world is more complex and diverse, mutually shaping and spontaneously changing
Vertical communication reinforces command and control	Horizontal communication fosters the free flow of information and collaboration
Focus is on problems and deficits	Focus is on solutions and strengths

My definition of leadership is not meant to be a pithy one-liner, but rather a statement that captures the *essence* of what I think is important for the *future of the planet and organisations*:

> *Leadership is a shared relationship, where people are positively influenced to mobilise themselves around their toughest challenges, in service of a mutual purpose consistent with fundamental values.*

Dee Hock perhaps sums up this definition when he says, "The most abundant, least expensive, and most constantly abused resource in the world is *human ingenuity*. The source of that abuse is mechanistic, Industrial Age, dominator concepts of organisations and the management practices they spawn." [7]

Everyone was born a leader – until we were sent to school and taught to *be* managed, *to* manage and *comply*. You will remember my opening story – you were either the leader or the follower. It was unheard of to have *two* leaders. Today, far too often, we manage things and people in exactly the same way, the way we've done it since the 19th century. It's time for a new reality.

The new paradigm is about tapping into the awesome potential that we all have, including the desire to make a significant contribution. This call for a new paradigm is beyond surviving to something much grander. Covey describes it as "tapping into the higher reaches of human genius and motivation." [3]

It is the intersection of people's *talents* (your natural gifts and strengths), *passion* (those things that naturally energise, excite and inspire you), needs (including what your organisation or the world needs from you) and *conscience* (what you know to be the right thing to do).

A new paradigm must place much more value and emphasis on leveraging strengths while managing around our weaknesses. For example, the positive psychology literature demonstrates that there is very little evidence to support the value of aspiring to become a "well-rounded" leader. No-one became extraordinary by trying to be good at everything. In organisations and in the community generally, we must each play a role to help people tap into their dormant or under-utilised talents and strengths. Covey sums it all up well when he says:

> *Leadership is when people communicate to others their worth and potential so clearly they will come to see it in themselves.*

Despite a person's accomplishments, it seems that all of us have got just a little (or a lot) of the *imposter syndrome* – a psychological phenomenon in which people are unable to internalise their accomplishments. I often mention this in programs and *without exception*, at least half the room will nod in agreement, laugh nervously or give me a meek smile when I mention it. The reason I mention this is because if leadership is truly about enabling others to succeed, then don't they deserve a fair dose of belief from those they work with?

I have been fortunate to have at least two work colleagues and friends in my life who have done exactly this – at different times, they both demonstrated a greater belief in my potential and capability than I had in myself. For example, one manager said, "Phil, I think you're cruising. You can be *anything* you want to be in this organisation, such is your potential." What do you think happened to my confidence and self-belief as a result? They changed the course of my career and life in a positive and inspiring way. What a simple, yet impactful leadership action. Has someone provided you with a similar gift? Or perhaps a more challenging question, have *you* provided such a gift?

What You Should Know About Leadership and Management Development

This is an exciting time to be a *leader* or, indeed, involved in developing our *leadership capability* for the next generation. No matter what your role, as a leader one of your primary responsibilities is to *develop the leadership capability of future generations*. Jack Welch of GE fame has been reported as saying that he used to dedicate at least 50 percent of his time to this critical task and has said, "Developing leaders is more important than developing strategy".

Critics of leadership and management development programs and culture change efforts argue that spending finite budgets on programs that normally don't show immediate benefits is a waste of money. On the contrary, developing your leadership and management capability, including a rich pipeline of talent, *could not be a better use of finite resources*. Building extraordinary leadership and management capacity is the future of any organisation.

It is also true that both management and leadership development go hand-in-hand, thus there are often benefits in incorporating management and leadership development programs together. After all, good leaders do not set aside their leadership skills when they focus on the managerial aspects of the enterprise, nor do good managers set aside their managerial skills when they focus on the leadership side of the enterprise. Since both can be extremely complex processes, it is often hard to say where one begins and the other one ends. [24]

I would like to provide several recommendations and guidelines (some from Rost [5]) for those responsible for leadership development programs:

- *Ensure leadership development doesn't occur in a vacuum.* Ensure that leadership and management development aligns with (1) a values-based culture (which *every* organisation should be striving for) and (2) is fit-for-purpose (for example, builds capacity to execute the organisation's strategy). *Leadership development needs to be framed and grounded in terms of the leader's biggest challenges, not an ephemeral burst of euphoria from short, superficial interventions.*

- *Always build organisational capacity around the Three Pillars of Performance.* Development programs need to be *always* firmly grounded within the Three Pillars of Performance: (1) *Capacity for Learning and Change,* (2) *Performance Alignment,* and (3) *Psychological Alignment.* If your development programs aren't grounded in the three pillars (or closely aligned principles), the return-on-investment you deserve probably won't be realised.

- *Ensure programs are well-balanced with a healthy bias on self-management.* The most effective programs teach participants as much about themselves as gaining valuable practical skills, including building trust, leading high performance teams and emotional intelligence (see the Seven Spheres of Leadership Mastery model in Part 4).

- *Involve key stakeholders in design.* As much as possible, involve relevant stakeholders in program design, including executive members, managers of participants (those who will be attending the program) and some of the participants themselves, to raise awareness, excitement and engagement. Depending on your organisation and situation, you may even consider obtaining customer input.

- *Stop focusing on the leader.* Leadership programs that only attempt to produce leader qualities among participants are less useful. Programs must reach well beyond emphasising leader traits, behaviours, and personal characteristics (Rost).

- *Prepare participants to use influence within non-coercive relationships.* Program activities should train participants to use persuasive and rational strategies of influence (Rost).

- *Help participants understand the nature of transformational change.* Leadership development programs should illustrate the key role organisational change plays in the post-industrial view of leadership. As change agents, participants should learn to challenge the status quo, create new visions, and sustain the movement (Rost).

- *Reconstruct participants' basic view toward a collaboration orientation.* Encourage participants to challenge the basic assumptions about life that are based on self-interest and competition. Leadership in the new millennium is much more collaborative and therefore leadership programs should encourage consensus, cooperation,

64

and collaboration rather than competition and unhelpful conflict (Rost).

If it is our goal to prepare those who work in our organisations, governments and communities, to lead effectively in the 21st century, then we must embrace this new paradigm in order to be successful in a world where rapid and constant change is the new 'status quo'. Our leadership programs should promote and foster learning, adaptability, openness, authenticity, and the skills required to live leadership as a relationship and shared journey. Anything less and we will be selling ourselves, our employees and society short.

Our leadership programs should promote and foster learning, adaptability, openness, authenticity, and the skills required to live leadership as a relationship and shared journey.

65

Part Four:

The Seven Spheres of Leadership Mastery

Chapter 9

The Seven Spheres of Leadership Mastery

If your actions inspire others to dream more, learn more, do more and become more, you are a leader.

John Quincy Adams, *(1767 – 1848), 6th US President*

A Leadership Development Framework

Figure 9.1 – The Seven Spheres of Leadership Mastery

The Seven Spheres of Leadership Mastery

The Seven Spheres of Leadership Mastery© is a central model used in our consulting practice, based on research, leadership theories and models and our own experience in working with leaders. It provides a touchstone for leadership development and practice rather than a definitive list of required qualities and attributes. The principles and depth that underpins each sphere, however, have helped thousands of leaders and organisations to be more successful. Based on each organisational context, strategy and challenges, programs are customised at the individual, team and organisational level. We have found that the seven spheres contribute very powerfully to many of the ideas and themes outlined in this book, so when you read them they may act as a summary of what you have read, rather than a lot of new information. What follows is a short description of each sphere, and then in Part 4, they are brought to life through a rolling case-study.

Manage and Lead Change

Key words: *agility, trusting self, manage and lead change, problem to an opportunity, learning, self-change, transition, systems intelligence.*

The ability to manage and lead change is an ongoing demand on leaders. There is nothing truer than the statement "change is constant". In fact, *disequilibrium is the new "normal"*. Research shows that the number one issue facing senior leaders is dealing with "adaptive challenges" and ambiguity.

Adaptive challenges can be defined as those *without* a defined solution, that require fundamental changes in values and beliefs and where there are often legitimate yet

...disequilibrium is the new "normal".

70

competing perspectives emerging. [11] Adaptive problems are often systemic problems with no ready answers and therefore systems intelligence (the ability to see the system and patterns of interdependence) can be useful. To effectively lead change in this environment, leaders need a special set of skills and a special approach. Skills include "getting on the balcony" (big picture perspective) and the ability to identify adaptive challenges (versus technical), regulating distress, maintaining disciplined attention, giving work back to where it belongs and protecting the voices of leadership below. [24]

Decisions about change also appear to cluster into two *archetypal theories and strategies for change*, both of which are not sufficient on their own. [17] Michael Beer calls them *Theory E*, which focuses on *creating economic value*, while *Theory O* focuses on *developing organisational capabilities and culture*. Leaders are encouraged to embrace the paradox sometimes created by both archetypes, called the *third strategic choice*. This integrative strategy has the benefits of short-term financial performance as well as long-term benefits of sustained change in all three pillars of performance.

Leaders are encouraged to embrace the paradox sometimes created by both archetypes, called the third strategic choice.

I am constantly surprised when working with organisations at how many senior people fail to consider both "E" and "O" strategies *concurrently*. A case-in-point was when I was working with a professional services firm in a number of areas, however primarily culture change. This particular HR Director insisted on telling me that the organisation needed to get a major systems implementation finalised *before* they could re-commence culture

71

change efforts. *What he failed to realise was that everything that happens in organisations – including behaviours, tolerated or not tolerated, system design, or policy and process improvement is a culture change opportunity. They are implicitly interdependent* – full stop.

Positive change requires *letting go of old patterns* and taking a fresh perspective. It includes a focus on opportunities rather than problems, long term versus short term and adaptability versus control.

Positive change requires letting go of old patterns and taking a fresh perspective.

It also invites us to move away from a *problem-centric focus* (that we love so much in organisations) to a *solution-centric focus*. Do you spend your energy and attention on what's not working, rather than on what you want to create in the future?

Action-Oriented

Key words: *coaching (self and others), potential, alignment, awareness-acceptance-commitment-action.*

The sound execution of strategy, combined with effective change management is essential for success. While many leaders and teams develop sound plans and strategies, few actually *execute* them effectively. Of particular concern is the notion of *entropy*, or a loss or leakage of energy in a system. This is where teams work on the *wrong things* or on the right things, but *ineffectively*. One top team I worked with became very excited by the Critical Success Factors (CSFs) that had been formulated at their team off-site.

Despite my recommendations to establish support mechanisms (that is, a *managed* project plan) to ensure they were properly implemented, the CEO failed to see the need. Twelve-months later, the team had barely moved on what they said a year earlier was "critical" to their success, and the business was languishing. While entropy can be minimised through alignment, too much alignment can actually have a *counter-productive effect*. Alignment shouldn't equal "frozen". In executing strategy or daily operations, there needs to be *adaptability and flexibility* built into the system, including a cultural norm that gives people permission at all levels to challenge and question the status quo.

Within this context, formal leaders need to create an environment where others can successfully align behaviours, symbols and systems to help ensure that valuable resources are used effectively and efficiently. Aligning people, processes and systems behind the vision also ensures sustainable and meaningful change in service of business goals — the holy grail of organisational success.

At the individual level, leadership is about creating a *safe* environment to enable others to fulfil their potential – in effect, *be their best*. It's about *coaching* others, rather than trying to control them, drawing out talents and strengths in service of team and organisational objectives. The Action Sphere is also about self-coaching, where we take responsibility for enhancing our own self-awareness, accepting new information, committing to change where appropriate, and then taking definitive and stepwise action towards the goal.

> *At the individual level, leadership is about creating a safe environment to enable others to fulfil their potential...*

73

Synergy

Key words: *relationships, collaboration, constructive conflict, managing teams, service, power, presence, emotional intelligence.*

Leaders create synergy by building meaningful relationships and high levels of trust. Importantly, research demonstrates that the most effective leaders have competencies in both *interpersonal* skills as well as a focus on *results.* [17] We also know that sometimes leaders must "give up" some of their "relational equity" *in service of something bigger.* Leaders need to be able to bring critical issues to the surface and deal with conflict constructively. Apart from courage, this requires leaders who are *emotionally intelligent* – highly self-aware and tuned into those around them.

Formal leaders also need to be able to make the shift from producing results to enabling and empowering others to produce the results. This is often a difficult transition for leaders to make because they need to let go of what made them successful in the past – technical competence. Once leaders begin to make this transition, they also begin to realise that the key role of leadership is to serve the needs of others' success, not the opposite. The shepherd exists for the sheep, not the other way around.

Navigating the "leadership transition" is one of the most common and most requested work we do with organisations that want to be build leadership capability. Whether it is partners in law and accounting firms, investment bankers or more generalist roles, making the transition from "technician"

74

to "leader" is difficult. I have found that a lot of the success we enjoy in supporting people to make this transition is to re-frame leadership around *key business challenges*. In other words, leadership development occurs in the context of their (work) reality, not in a vacuum. New leaders and "high potentials" begin to clearly see how they can lead effectively *and* leverage their technical skills concurrently. *Leadership*, however, becomes their new benchmark of "success".

Underpinning the sphere of synergy is the power of presence – the quality of absolute attention and listening. Presence can inspire and energise others and help them realise their potential.

Presence can inspire and energise others and help them realise their potential.

Truth

Key words: *purpose, values, legacy, talents, strengths, making a difference, authenticity.*

Truth is about connecting with our purpose, values and core strengths in areas that make a difference. Purpose is not a goal or the latest "fad", it's something leaders need to discover and is beyond our job or even career. It includes a "reason for being" that drives action beyond oneself. It is only with this clarity that extraordinary performance can occur, both in business and personal arenas. *Values,* on the other hand, are the standards and guiding principles that govern our lives.

In my experience, values are often *talked about* in organisations, particularly when everything is going well. But when there are real business challenges

75

to confront, values are the *last* thing to be considered. I had the pleasure of working with a Managing Director in the Asia Pacific region who was an exception. She would regularly talk about the organisational values *and* use them as a reference in making tough decisions. Sometimes the values clashed directly with each other (for example, *customer* and *shareholder*), but it was the *robust conversations* surrounding the values that made the team's decision making processes so effective.

Strengths enable us to be our best by leveraging what we're good at and extinguishing our weaknesses. *Truth* means being congruent and *authentic* in service of what we believe in as leaders. These three domains form a powerful coalition. [26]

Inspiring leaders openly communicate their principles and what they stand for despite their popularity. Most importantly, they model the behaviours required to move towards a high performance culture. They truly "walk the talk" in everything they do. If you influence the lives of those around you, you are engaged in the act of leadership and each of us is creating a legacy as we live our lives. Our *leadership legacy* is the sum total of the difference we make in people's lives. Many leaders fail to consciously craft their legacy, instead leaving it to chance.

> *Most importantly, they (leaders) model the behaviours required to move towards a high performance culture.*

Engage

Key words: *vision, future-orientation, goals, inspire, storytelling.*

76

Leaders need to be able to create a compelling vision, or picture of the future, that creates a highly focused, results-driven culture. An organisation's vision needs to be a picture that energises people rather than just a "let's-go-through-the-motions" type statement. Telling the story about a *compelling* mission, vision and values can energise entire organisations when done well. While most leaders love to make strategy, it is a well crafted vision and supporting values that spawn strategic action. The absence of a vision will doom any strategy – especially a strategy for change.

Do you want to encourage extraordinary performance? Do you want people to do great things? If the answer is "yes", then create a culture that inspires, empowers and energises people. People will only do what they have to do for a manager who does not display leadership, but they will always give their best for a manager who is a real leader. To inspire, you must both create resonance and move people with a compelling vision. You must embody what you ask of others and be able to articulate a shared vision in a way that inspires others to act. You must offer a sense of common purpose beyond the day-to-day tasks, making work exciting and fun.

While being an inspiring leader is insufficient on its own, those who are able to connect powerfully with people are at a distinct advantage. Often people can feel inspired in unexpected or counter-intuitive ways. It is not the heroic leader who usually inspires others, but rather the "simple" human actions such as authenticity, empathy, or a powerful personal story. These qualities can be used to mobilise people, connect with others, and build quality relationships.

Resilience

Key words: *energy management, wellbeing, optimism, stress management, exercise.*

Sound energy management practices help people to achieve sustained performance, energy and enjoyment. Traditional views have addressed only parts of the energy management equation. Sound energy management means addressing *all four domains* effectively – physical, emotional, mental and spiritual (head, heart, body, meaning). A very simple personal story will help illustrate the power of tapping into these energy sources for ourselves and others.

When my son Thomas was about nine years old and at primary school, each morning we had to go through a *protracted and frustrating* ritual of waking him up from a deeper sleep than Sleeping Beauty. On Saturday nights, however, he would sleep dressed *in* his football gear (except boots) to "save time" on Sunday mornings – so he wouldn't be late for football. Thomas would get up at around *5 am* (strangely *unassisted*) on Sunday morning to get ready for football (usually *waking us* at around 6 am) for football at 9 am. This is the power of the fourth energy source – spiritual (purpose and meaning). Can you imagine the power of tapping into this energy source for yourself and those in your organisation?

Energy management is not limited to oneself, and effective leaders also know how to unlock energy and potential in others through an empowering, strengths-based approach. The field of positive psychology holds significant promise for how we manage and lead in organisations. The Values-in-Action (VIA) survey is a great starting point to think about your own strengths and how to leverage them.

While "life balance" remains distinctly individual, having the requisite skills to manage all four domains is fundamental to sustained, high performance. In today's fast-paced world, where it feels like we're being pulled in many different directions, energy management and building resourcefulness are critical.

You

Key words: *character, authenticity, self-change, beliefs, self-awareness.*

Many people tend to split the act of leadership from the person, whereas the two are inseparable. We also tend to see leadership as an external event – something we do. Leadership, however, comes from a *deeper reality* – it comes from our values, principles, life experiences and essence. It is a *whole-of-person* action. We lead by virtue of who we are – this is real leadership (or leadership from the inside out). Fundamental to the most effective, results-producing leaders are *authenticity; influence and value creation.* [25]

Our definition of leadership is that it is a *shared relationship, where people are positively influenced to mobilise themselves around their toughest challenges, in service of a mutual purpose consistent with fundamental values.*

Leadership can come from our character, the essence of who we are – or it can come from a pattern of coping, where we tend to react to circumstances to elicit an immediate result. Character is the *essence* of a leader and works to *transform* and open up possibilities and potential, while coping protects us and

Character is the essence of a leader and works to transform and open up possibilities and potential...

79

helps us get through challenging circumstances. If used sparingly, it has value. The coping leader may get results, but also exhibit defensiveness, fear, withdrawal, or a desire to win at all costs — all things that *diminish* performance. [26]

Like most people who have worked in organisations for a period of time, I have experienced both "character-based" leaders and "coping-based" leaders. Those who lead through character are generally those who also manage "task" and "relationship" most effectively.

I recently had the pleasure of coaching a CEO from a not-for-profit organisation who was the *epitome* of a *character-based leader.* He consciously focused on living in accord with his principles and values. He had a deep sense of purpose and legacy, and cared about the community and the role of his organisation within it. He was not threatened by those in his executive team or more broadly who demonstrated superior knowledge, skills or experience to his own.

His belief in people and his role in developing them is captured in a quote from Wilma Rudolph (1940-1994), who was the first American woman runner to win three gold medals at a single Olympics.

She said:
Never underestimate the power of dreams and the influence of the human spirit. We are all the same in this notion: The potential for greatness lives within each of us.

Chapter 10

Leadership in Practice

Leadership and learning are indispensable to each other.

John Fitzgerald Kennedy *(1917-1963), 35th US President*

Maintain and Develop Systems Intelligence

We have now discussed a number of trends and themes surrounding the current industrial age leadership paradigm. I have called for a shift from the current paradigm to a new paradigm based on relationships, empowerment, autonomy, adaptability and action. So it is now time to outline what we can do in a practical sense to bring a new paradigm to life.

Systems intelligence is the ability to see the systems and patterns of interdependence within organisations and beyond. [26] Once people start to see the systemic patterns, early action can be taken. Edgar Shein believes human systems are essentially *role networks*, and one must learn to influence roles more than people. [22] In the work we do with leaders, either in a one-on-one coaching capacity, leadership or team development, we use *systems maps* and *role analysis* extensively. Focusing on role and the

"Focusing on role and the role an individual is playing can be extraordinarily powerful."

83

role an individual is playing can be extraordinarily powerful.

For example, when working with an executive team, one member drew his systems map using the metaphor of a car, *with him as the brake!* This created a rich discussion about the role that person felt they needed to take up to protect the organisation from undue risk. It created a major breakthrough in the team as they were able to have a deep discussion about the issue and move to a whole new plane of performance.

Give the Work Back to the People Who Have the Problem

I remember coaching a new Chairman of a large Australian-based organisation. During the discussion he outlined to me how he had scheduled a "meet and greet' tour of all their offices around the country. During the tour, he intended to talk to as many staff as possible to get their views on what was happening in the firm – both good and bad. Good so far, right? When I asked him the purpose of doing that, he said that this would enable him to work out all the things *he* needed to do to fix the organisation (along with the CEO and her team).

The Chairman was about to fall into the common trap of shouldering the burden of all the ills of the organisation. While he certainly has a responsibility and, along with the CEO, is ultimately accountable, this doesn't mean he had to take on the responsibility of fixing it single-handedly – an impossible task.

The Chairman was about to fall into the common trap of shouldering the burden of all the ills of the organisation.

84

We then discussed some simple strategies such as:

- When asking people what's not working, ask them what they have tried in the past to make progress on the problem.
- Ask them what support they need from you to make this happen.
- Ask them what type of organisation they would like to help create.

Listen to Those Who *Don't* Sing from the Same Page

Edgar Shein once wrote, "Organisations are coercive systems." [22] They tend to reinforce a party line, so listening to the periphery, those who do not share the views of the mainstream, is a skill leaders will need more and more as there will be limited understanding, at best, of the forces shaping culture. [4] Heifetz and Laurie also talk about "protecting the leadership voices from below". [23]

They generate disequilibrium and the best way for organisations to silence them is to neutralise them...

Whistle-blowers, creative deviants and those who call attention to things people would rather ignore, *are routinely smashed and silenced in organisations.* They generate disequilibrium, and the best way for companies to silence them is to neutralise them, often in the name of "alignment" or teamwork. I have regularly heard CEOs and other senior members *deride* certain vocal members in their businesses. These vocal individuals may well be speaking directly to systemic issues that need to be addressed.

85

Create Psychological Safety

Psychological safety is where employees at any level feel they can challenge the status quo without negative consequences. In the leadership programs we run, we usually talk about what people fear most in demonstrating real leadership in their respective teams and organisation. There are many common elements and, interestingly, it doesn't matter at what level of the organisation, we hear much the same thing including:

- "I'll lose my job."
- "My performance review (and therefore my remuneration and/or incentives) may be negatively affected."
- "My boss will make life difficult for me." (including CEOs)
- "People won't like me."
- "I'll be branded a troublemaker," or some variation on these themes.

Creating high levels of trust and safety are therefore critical.

Creating high levels of trust and safety are therefore critical.

Create and Regulate Disequilibrium

As mentioned a number of times, a key part of a leader's role is to create and regulate distress. Adaptive work generates distress, but there should be a balance between people being in 'sleep mode' and feeling so *distressed* that they become non-productive and wracked with fear and self-preservation. Heifetz, Grashow and Linsky call it *productive disequilibrium,* where people feel the heat of change but are still able to function well to make progress on the challenge before them. [11] They recommend leaders attend to three fundamental tasks in order to help maintain a productive level of tension:

- Create what can be called a holding environment (like a pressure cooker, where the heat and pressure are regulated).
- Be responsible for direction, protection, orientation, managing conflict, and shaping norms.
- Maintain presence and poise (regulating distress is perhaps a leader's most difficult job).

If You're Going to Manage Anyone, Manage Yourself

In modern organisations, where sometimes progress is rewarded at any cost, internal competition is high, political game playing is the norm, and people feel the need to engage in self-protective behaviours (for example, passive-aggressive or passive-defensive behaviours), being oneself can be a challenge. Remaining open and authentic, however, is critical in the workplace, whether you are a formal leader or not.

Remaining open and authentic, however, is critical in the workplace, whether you're a formal leader or not.

This is a view shared by many researchers and writers. Dee Hock, for example, says that the "first and paramount responsibility of anyone who purports to manage is to manage self: one's own integrity, character, ethics, knowledge, wisdom, temperament, words, and acts." [7] We spend little time and rarely excel at management of self precisely because it is so much more difficult than prescribing and controlling the behaviour of others. Hock continues to say, however, that without management of self, no one is fit for authority no matter how much they acquire; for the more authority they acquire the more dangerous they become. Practically, this is about saying what is really on our minds, sharing our fears and concerns at the appropriate time, and not pretending to be something we're not. It can be enormously liberating, particularly in teams, when the team moves to a whole new level of realness. I've regularly seen huge gains in cooperation, trust, communication and, importantly, performance.

There is no doubt that changing paradigms is very difficult. To move to a new paradigm, we must all *let go of antiquated models* that do not serve us very well in the 21st century. It means moving from authority-based management and behaviours to shared leadership. Hock says, "The problem is that nothing else is going to work. We have tried all the easy ways – the one-minute leader, situational, contingency, great person, nice guy/tough guy trait approaches – and they don't work. So maybe it is time to get serious and try the difficult but more promising approach. It is time to move from an understanding of leadership centered on the individual to one centered on a relationship." [7]

Nothing I am proposing changes the nature of accountability. Those in

Paradoxically, giving away control by increasing autonomy increases accountability...

formal authority positions need to maintain 100 percent accountability for the actions and decisions of people who report to them in some way. Paradoxically, *giving away control by increasing autonomy increases accountability* as people need to think more independently and make decisions accordingly.

88

The Seven Spheres of

Leadership Mastery

in Practice

Chapter 11

Manage and Lead Change

Two-thirds of all change initiatives fail. This is a sobering fact for all managers and leaders in organisations. A case in point is a senior executive called Robert Dale from Asia Pacific Inc.* Robert needed to change the organisation's culture to meet the needs of the newly developed strategy.

As CEO, Robert needed everyone in the organisation – not just those in formal leadership positions – to be *engaged* in the change process, actively working to reduce inefficient processes, and address poor customer service and the subsequent below par financial results.

On the surface and according to most management texts, Robert did everything right. He knew that he had to create a *compelling story*, because employees must see the point of the change and agree with it.

* Robert and Asia Pacific Inc are pseudonyms however Robert is a composite of real leaders.

Robert discussed the need to *role model* the new behaviours with his executive team and the need to align reinforcing mechanisms such as systems, processes, and incentives. Robert consulted with his HR department to ensure that relevant development programs were put in place to build capability so employees would have the skills required to make the desired changes.

After 12 months had passed, and after spending a lot of time, energy and money, the *change outcomes remained patchy and isolated.* The strategy also remained a *theoretical framework* for change. Customer service remained low, and in some cases there was evidence that employees were actively resisting the change. By any measure, the change had failed and the organisation was now *vulnerable to competitive forces.*

So what went wrong? There were a number of fatal errors. Robert had failed to take into account contemporary insights about human nature – insights that if not carefully considered will get in the way of applying the necessary conditions required for meaningful, positive change.

Firstly, what often motivates you doesn't motivate most of your employees. What the leader cares about (and typically bases at least 80 percent of his or her message to others on) does not tap into roughly 80 percent of the workforce's primary motivators for putting extra energy into the change program.

Well-intentioned leaders invest significant time in communicating their change story. While this is necessary, more time should be invested in listening, not telling, and involving employees in the conversation about

94

the change. We also know that many leaders focus their story on the *deficit-approach* or the burning platform. While this may appeal to some employees, many are looking for a *positive* reason to change – for example, what the organisation is trying to create.

In terms of role-modelling appropriate behaviours, leaders believe mistakenly that they already "are the change". Robert believed he had built a *high-trust environment*. However, his mixed messages to different executives, effectively "playing them off each other" *destroyed trust*. The ripple effect was felt throughout the entire organisation.

Executives often commit to role modelling constructive behaviours – and then, in practice, nothing significant changes. *The reason for this is that most executives don't count themselves among the ones who need to change.* How many executives would answer "no" to the question, "Are you a team-player?" and "yes" to the question "Are you a blocker?" The answer is *none*. The fact is that human beings consistently think they are *better* than they are and others are *worse* than they actually are. We judge ourselves by our *intentions* and others by their *actions*.

Robert also failed to adequately motivate and energise people around the change. There are also many myths about reinforcing mechanisms and what motivates people. For example, money is *the* most expensive motivator, while small, unexpected rewards can pay for themselves *many times over*. Any change also needs to be perceived as fair – reality doesn't actually matter, it's what employees *think* that matters.

Many of the problems Robert faced were systemic and adaptive – that is, those without a defined solution that required fundamental changes in values, beliefs, priorities and loyalties. Legitimate, yet competing perspectives emerged and Robert's formal leaders were not adequately prepared or skilled to deal with them effectively. They were used to applying quick technical fixes to issues that needed to be explored more deeply so that meaningful progress could be made.

To effectively lead change in this environment, leaders need a special approach and set of skills. Skills include systems intelligence, the ability to actually identify the adaptive component of their various challenges, being able to turn the heat up and down as required and maintaining disciplined attention on the change process. They failed on almost every count because they were used to operating from an old "command and control", linear doctrine.

To avoid being one of the two-thirds of projects that fail, positive change requires letting go of old patterns and taking a fresh perspective. It includes a focus on opportunities rather than problems, long-term versus short-term thinking, and building adaptability versus controlling people and things.

Chapter 12

Action-Orientation

In an attempt to catch up to competitors, Asia Pacific Inc needed new growth. The strategy needed to allow API to improve its innovation capability and get crucial products and services to market quicker than its competitors.

Robert instructed his executive team to formulate project teams that would allow API to review its business practices, policies, procedures and culture to support the new strategy. Three project teams were formulated, each headed by one of the three divisional heads. After six months, it was clear that each of the teams was *burning money and using valuable resources*. Progress was negligible, and in some cases, more problems had been encountered than solutions.

Taking the wrong action in organisations is endemic – and the evidence is overwhelming. A study conducted by John Kotter in 1996 and more recent research conducted by McKinsey, show that *seven out of ten* change efforts *fail*. How can this be so? More importantly, how much money is mismanagement of change costing *your* organisation? The figure may well frighten you, but as a rough estimate, calculate the cost of everyone in your company who is working on changing behaviours, systems, processes or structures and then assume that *70 percent of that figure is money down the drain.* No organisation can afford this – it *is* costing you dearly.

So what went wrong with the three project teams appointed by Robert? The problem literally started at the *top*. While a growth strategy had been formulated, it was a poor plan put together by Robert and one member of the team (who had "strategy" as part of their portfolio). The document had been discussed three times by the entire executive team, with each discussion lasting a couple of hours. While Robert believed that executive team members were provided with ample opportunities to debate the strategy and provide input, the reality in the team's mind was very different. As I have seen dozens of times, most members of the executive did not feel they debated the pros and cons of the strategy at all – in fact, half the team thought it was the *wrong* strategy altogether, but failed to speak up strongly enough to be heard.

So why didn't seasoned executives speak up and challenge Robert and each other? *They simply didn't feel safe to do so.* In the back of their minds they remember the executive who was asked to leave last year, who, in their view, was the only one who *challenged* Robert regularly. Whether this is the real reason he was asked to leave doesn't matter – *perception is reality*. Because executive team members didn't have "buy in" to the strategy (at best) and disagreed and even undermined the strategy (at worst), the project teams were actually *impotent*. Despite his good intentions, Robert had provided *counterfeit* and *myopic leadership* by expecting project teams to come up with the answers when he, as the CEO, hadn't laid a solid foundation. The resulting entropy was causing the organisation to *increase* the rate of deterioration, rather than *arrest* it.

Other initiatives implemented were also largely impotent. To start with, the culture change project hinged on a diagnosis done internally by people with an overly simplistic understanding of culture. The diagnosis was flawed in its design and failed to uncover key legacy issues. Other examples of largely impotent actions that in some cases were downright destructive included poorly managed restructures (used as a band-aid and not addressing the intended issues); trotting out familiar training programs that didn't challenge the status quo; defining the challenge to fit the current expertise; and simply denying some of the key problems within Asia Pacific Inc actually existed.

What could Robert have done differently? Robert *and* his executive team needed to role model the aspirational culture by encouraging and having crucial conversations, building trust and listening to the challenges people faced at all levels of the organisation. There is no doubt that Robert could have helped people face reality as it related to their condition, threats and opportunities. He needed to effectively *mobilise* the organisation to do adaptive work and adjust their values, habits, practices and priorities. Real leaders also take responsibility for being the source of the movement, rather than waiting for other people.

At the individual level, it is about creating a safe environment to enable others to fulfil their potential – in effect, be their best. It's about coaching others rather than trying to control them, drawing out talents and strengths in service of team and organisational objectives. Leaders need to have high levels of self-awareness and the ability to *create tension* at the right time and with the right people to overcome *inertia*.

Also, had Robert supported the change agenda with *team and individual coaching*, he would have found that people and teams would have taken responsibility for change at all levels of the organisation. People would have been more accepting of new information, demonstrated higher levels of commitment to change and then taken definitive and stepwise action towards the goal.

People would have been focused and energised on creating a company that was "fit-for-purpose" for the strategic objectives. There would have been no wasted energy on activities and tasks that kept everybody busy but didn't really achieve much. *To do anything else is a costly and largely futile exercise.*

Chapter 13

Synergy

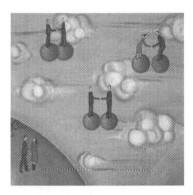

Synergy simply means that the effect of the whole is greater than the sum of the effects of the individual parts. In undertaking any initiative, particularly formulating strategy and building a "fit-for-purpose" and values-based culture, creating synergy is a must-have. Synergy, in an organisational sense, means building relationships, enabling a collaborative environment, creating constructive conflict to tease out people's real views and manage and lead teams effectively.

Robert and the executive team demonstrated poor skills in helping to provide an environment based on *real relationships*. Robert was "old-school" in fostering competition amongst his team in the false belief it created higher levels of performance. This competition created a silo mentality between key divisions and ultimately led to lower levels of overall performance.

The culture at API was also very command and control-oriented, where people were expected to comply with managerial expectations without making a fuss. This translated into a toxic culture of high avoidance and compliance; passivity, approval-seeking, and aggressive behaviours. One of the cultural norms that existed within the organisation was that managers were the "boss" because they had more experience and therefore knew the right actions to take. Many managers within API, including CEO Robert, prided themselves on being no-nonsense leaders. They were often hard on their people to get results, a practice that was overlooked most of the time because they "met their numbers". The story within the organisation was that "until someone tells me I should behave differently, I'll continue to manage how I choose".

Numbers-driven leaders are often seen as results driven and good for business, but they are hardly *ever* good for business in the medium to long term. *They effectively burn people.* They fail to balance the pragmatic and necessary focus on results with the necessary second face or dimension – people. It is a cliché to say that people are an organisation's most important resource – but even this statement misses the point – people *are* your organisation, not just a resource!

Just because the CEO didn't seem to have a problem with a "no-nonsense" numbers-driven leadership style, didn't mean *it* wasn't a problem – there was indeed a cost. Many people *hated* working there and turnover was higher than in most of their peer organisations. Many talented people only stayed for a short period and it had always been hard to attract good people. Engagement scores had also just about bottomed out, indicating some serious problems.

Effective leaders, or more to the point – true leaders, are able to build relationships and high performance teams in service of organisational goals, not despite them. *Long-term sustainable performance requires people at all levels of the organisation to be engaged and focused on the job at hand.* They need to feel like their opinion counts, that they have a say in how things are run and that the organisation does have their interests at heart, not just "hitting the numbers".

People need to be able to *feel* the values and good intentions of those in formal positions of authority. Employees need to know (and see) leaders serving those in the organisation who actually do the work – usually those closest to the customer. *Senior leaders exist to make others more successful, not the other way around!*

Two key attributes of effective leaders are *emotional intelligence* and *presence.* Emotionally intelligent leadership would dictate that Robert and senior managers (as a minimum) at Asia Pacific Inc demonstrate empathy, self-awareness, and the ability to manage their own emotions and control responses, particularly when feeling threatened or when under stress. Presence on the other hand is the ability to be completely present and *fully attend* to those around you. A practical example of *not* being present is when people continue typing while talking to others, fiddle with their phones while pretending to listen, or simply thinking about something else unrelated to the conversation. Being fully present can be wonderfully inspirational and rapidly build credibility and relationships.

Leaders like Robert and his team need to understand that leadership is not an individualistic exercise, but rather a shared and co-created one. They need to be able to put their egos aside at times and let others "step up" and lead, particularly those who are in the best position to voice a view based on where and what they do, not their formal position in the hierarchy. This may mean, for example, that a graduate may have more answers than the CEO in some circumstances.

To create synergy, leaders need to be able to *surface and manage conflict constructively* and create safety for people to talk about the real issues, no matter how uncomfortable this may be at times. Leaders need to be able to manage both "cool" and "hot" topics within the team. Cool topics have more certainty, more available data and therefore usually lower levels of emotion. Hot topics, on the other hand, can usually be characterised by being more subjective, often with no readily available answers (for example, adaptive challenges), are hard to test, have higher levels of emotions and disagreement and therefore they often get "personal".

Paradoxically, effective leaders sometimes need to *provoke* the system — for example, a team — to overcome inertia. For instance, the much vaunted former leader of GE, Jack Welch, talked about how when he first arrived at GE his new management team had an air of "superficial congeniality". In other words, it was an ineffective team that thought being nice to each other was being a high performance team. To provoke the system Jack Welch used to *throw "hand grenades"*, metaphorically speaking of course, to surface the real issues.

So in summary, effective leaders must be able to demonstrate competencies in both *interpersonal skills* as well as a focus on *results*. They must have high levels of self-awareness, as well as being able to read situations and other people well. They must also be able to use their own emotions in an *intelligent way*. They must be authentic and demonstrate core personal and organisational values, not just talk about them. Leaders like Robert must be able to build and maintain relationships with factions or groups with different interests and agendas to his own. This is the work of *real leadership*.

Chapter 14

Truth

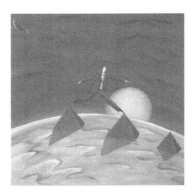

In many ways children know a lot about leadership. Children seem to have a gift for telling it *as it is* – in effect expressing what they're thinking and feeling. My children, for example, don't mind telling me that they don't like what I'm wearing or that when I say something they don't agree with that "I'm just being silly". Not that I'm suggesting we should adopt this exact approach in organisations.

Truth and authenticity in leadership are sadly often missing in organisations. Yet when it is demonstrated, people usually connect with the person in unexpected ways. Let's return to Robert, our hapless CEO whose organisation, API, needs to formulate and execute a new strategy just to keep up with its competitors. So far, little progress has been made in surfacing the real issues where progress needs to be made or in building a constructive culture to serve the strategy.

Earlier, we discussed that Robert had (on the surface at least) done a number of things right – one of these being his road shows. However, the way he went about selling his vision was flawed. Robert was not driven by a strong *sense of purpose* around the strategy or the organisation – and this came through during his presentations. They were largely lifeless, data-heavy PowerPoint presentations that *failed to engage people* in the most fundamental of ways – at the levels of *head, heart, hands and spirit* (purposefulness). The "killer blow" for Robert was that he failed to speak the truth and tell it "as it was". Instead, he made a number of references to external factors and how difficult it had been for him and the executive. At no time did he take responsibility for their lacklustre performance. Worse still, Robert had not learnt how to speak authentically and simply *be* authentic. *The art of telling a powerful story can move the most resistant and cynical person if crafted correctly.* When listening to him, people weren't sure whether to believe him or not.

I will share a very simple example which demonstrates the converse of Robert and a story that has stuck with me over a long period of time. Some years ago I was running a leadership program for a group of banking people in their twenties and thirties – a mixed lot of marketing professionals, analysts, and managers. I asked the question, "Who do you find most inspiring as a leader?" The reply was revealing – they went on to describe a senior woman (let's call her Christine) within the organisation (around 40,000 people) and it was what Christine *did* that I found to be the most surprising. When I asked why they (almost all) had chosen her, they said that on a recent visit to their interstate office, this executive had spent time walking around and chatting to people, asking them what they did and what were their challenges. Expecting them to finish with a heroic leadership story, they said what they found inspiring was that she *cared* and took the time to talk to them as people. She was *interested* in them and showed that *their* goals were more important than *hers*.

How do you think her department performed? Exceptionally well. Her simple yet powerful style – "What you say matters, what you think matters, and I'm here to support you" – *demonstrated that people matter*. Upon further investigation, however, she did a lot more.

Christine did what children do so well – *she was real*. In developing and leading her 3,000-odd staff, she would focus on *positive change* by constantly reminding people of why they were there and where they were heading. There we no great speeches seeking to enhance her own status and ego. Instead, she focused on simple yet powerful stories about customers who had received service beyond what was expected and what it meant to them. She sometimes asked customers to come in and meet staff who would normally never come into contact with customers (usually her own senior people!). *She focused on what was working in the business and people's strengths rather than weaknesses*. Weaknesses were not ignored but largely extinguished through smart management.

Christine constantly talked about *values* – both her own values and the stated organisational values. She backed up this talk through constant demonstration of a commitment to the values. For example, in making decisions in her team she would foster meaningful (and often tough) conversations about the pros and cons of a decision, taking into

109

consideration the business objectives, shareholders, customers and staff. *Values were used as a touchstone for all decisions. Is this the right thing to do?*

Inspiring leaders openly communicate their principles and what they stand for *despite their popularity*. Most importantly, they model the behaviours required to move towards a high performance culture. They truly walk the talk in everything they do.

Her team always got a sense of purpose (and urgency) from Christine which was infused throughout her department. People felt like they were engaged in work that mattered. While everyone worked very hard, they could see beyond themselves and were reminded of the bigger picture. Their contribution was recognised formally and informally on a regular basis.

Christine also understood one key thing – and that was that *leadership is about creating leadership* in others – not doing it *to* them. She largely didn't buy into the 'leader-follower' paradigm, knowing that this can create enormous dependence, inertia and underperformance in organisations. Christine and her management team knew that to achieve their stretch goals consistently – year in, year out – they could not afford to manage and lead in a top-down traditional way. *People had to understand where they were going and why.* It was then the job of senior management to help create the conditions that enabled people to take ownership and accountability for their results at all levels of the department. They did this through three vehicles: by encouraging people to take action at the local level; by providing a culture where it was okay to speak up and challenge; and finally by supporting people to be their best.

Underpinning all of this, however, was a sense of authenticity. People always knew where they stood with Christine. Far from being a wilting flower, she was not afraid to have the tough conversations. The difference was that she did this in a very constructive way. Her leadership team was also a place where its members knew they could have real conversations – not conversations sanitised by the weight of expectation about how a team was meant to have conversations. *Conflict was not only managed, it was encouraged.* Issues that lay below the surface that could damage the team and the organisation were surfaced and dealt with. As a consequence, trust levels were high and people in the team knew that each member had their eye on the collective, not the individual prize. Christine rewarded this behaviour and actively discouraged individualistic behaviour.

Christine's leadership style also created an atmosphere of commitment. When a decision was made, the team got right behind it and committed to a plan of action. Even if some people disagreed with the decision, the very fact that they had been heard on the issue allowed them to accept it. They held each other accountable for collective results and didn't tolerate anything less. All the conversations in the team were authentic. She also knew that there was actually no such thing as a dysfunctional team or department – in that each was perfectly aligned to get the results it got. They actively worked on aligning the team for achievement and success.

Christine and her team also realised that once they were able to positively influence the lives of those around them, then they would be engaged in the act of leadership and each of them would be, in effect, creating a legacy. *Our leadership legacy is the sum total of the difference we make in people's lives.* Many leaders fail to consciously craft their legacy, instead leaving it to chance. Christine knew that she wanted to leave the organisation much stronger and self-sufficient than when she arrived. By being true to ourselves and the organisational mission, we set up a foundation for success. That brings us back to children and what they can teach us about leadership. While strategy and vision-setting are important, it's only part of the story.

Children can teach us that to be a successful leader we need to be real – real in our relationships, real in how we interact and real about what we think people most need in organisations. Today people need a more humanistic environment where they can be their best in service of business goals and an organisational mission they care about. Robert, and many leaders like him, could to take a leaf out of Christine's book.

Chapter 15

Engage

Leaders need to be able to create a compelling vision, or picture of the future, that creates a highly focused, results-driven culture. Robert failed to engage his own team and the organisation more broadly. While most leaders love to make strategy, it's vision and values that will doom a strategy. An organisation's vision needs to be a picture that energises people rather than just a "let's-go-through-the-motions" type statement.

A true vision shapes all activities, including recruitment and selection, reward and recognition, and how customers, shareholders and suppliers are treated. In today's chaotic world, and aligned to the principles of adaptive leadership, leaders should also be encouraged to adopt a more experimental approach to strategic planning, running multiple-micro strategies and then adapting resource allocation according to effectiveness.

Again, Robert and the executive team failed to engage in robust debate about the best way forward and therefore didn't formulate or articulate a coherent strategy that moved the organisation forward.

One of the interesting peculiarities about engaging people in change and implementation of strategy is that we actually often know *what* needs to be done, but we don't do it. One of the reasons is that the rewards for changing are some time away in the future, while the discomfort, disequilibrium and pain have to be dealt with *now*. Leaders like Robert therefore have to guide, encourage, support and manage the disequilibrium over the short and medium term.

In terms of values, companies that have strong values are often more successful than those that don't. In high performing companies, values guide behaviour and decision making. Those who don't behave in accord with organisational values need to receive remedial development and ultimately be asked to leave the organisation if there is not sufficient improvement. As Jack Welch says, you must be public about the consequences of breaching core values. When you announce simply that an executive has "left to pursue other business interests," you lose the chance to make a statement about values.

Robert needed to employ a disciplined approach to Asia Pacific Inc's vision and values. They guide everyone in the organisation about *what* needs to be delivered, *how* it needs to be delivered and *why*. One international company I worked with assessed every manager according to two criteria – their current *performance* and their *values*. This company, as do others, used

114

a nine-cell matrix with performance on one axis and values on the other. In a general sense, those who "lived the values" but whose performance was not up to scratch, were given intensive support to improve. Conversely, high performers whose behaviours did not meet the standards demanded by the values, were also given intensive support; however, if they didn't improve their behaviours, they were asked to leave or were terminated.

Telling the story about a compelling mission, vision and values can energise entire organisations when done well. A key skill of leadership is to be able to influence others. Storytelling can take many shapes – from "water-cooler conversations" to personal stories, to large scale town-hall type addresses – and is a key leadership tool. According to Craig Wortmann, [27] stories:

- create leadership *presence*.
- create a context for listeners.
- build relationships.
- illustrate success and failure.
- allow reflection.
- act as an antidote from data and information overload.
- show us the how, what and why.
- show multiple perspectives.
- help us *unlearn* bad habits and *behaviours*, and
- spread beyond their immediate audiences.

I have found that many leaders lack the self-confidence and know-how to tell powerful, effective stories. However, with a relatively small amount of training, combined with some simple processes to gain clarity about the mission, vision and values, leaders become very excited at being able to

115

tell a great business-related story people remember and talk about. After only a small amount of coaching, a CEO I was working with changed his approach and style substantially regarding a major announcement, with excellent outcomes.

Chapter 16

Resilience

After a year of spinning the wheels at API, Robert was feeling despondent. His revitalisation of API was a dismal failure, slipping further behind the competition with levels of engagement across the organisation at an *all-time low*.

After working extremely hard over a number of years, combined with the poor shape of API, he was starting to think that perhaps it all wasn't worth it. He was starting to ask the hard questions about his working life – actually, his life generally. He had risen to CEO of API at a relatively young age, but his sense of enjoyment and fulfilment he got from work had all but *disappeared*. He wasn't sleeping well – often waking in the middle of the night thinking about his "to do" list. He was eating poorly and was 10 kilograms overweight. He was snappy with people around him, including his family. He pronounced, "Why can't they understand how much pressure I'm under?!"

Does any of this sound or feel familiar? Can you see some of yourself in Robert? We live in a global village connected by digital media. Our pace is rushed, rapid-fire, and relentless. Facing crushing workloads, we try to cram as much as possible into every day. *Time management is no longer a viable solution.* We need more. It's also not about 'coping' or 'surviving' – this is a state of mind which is not helpful. We shouldn't just "get by" – it's not fair to our work colleagues or the organisation and it's not fair to our family and friends. Most importantly, however, you deserve more.

According to the American Psychological Association:

Resilience is the process of adapting well in the face of adversity, trauma, tragedy, threats, or even significant sources of stress – such as family and relationship problems, serious health problems, or workplace and financial stressors. It means "bouncing back" from difficult experiences. [28]

Resilience is not a trait that people either have or do not have. It involves behaviours, thoughts, and actions that can be learned and developed in anyone.

A combination of factors contributes to resilience:
- caring and supportive relationships.
- the capacity to make realistic plans and take steps to carry them out.

118

- a positive view of yourself and confidence in your strengths and abilities.
- skills in communication and problem solving.
- the capacity to manage strong feelings and impulses.

All of these are factors that people can develop in themselves. Some of the strategies Robert could consider to build resilience include [1]:

- *making connections.* Good relationships with close family members, friends, or others are important.
- *avoiding seeing crises as insurmountable problems.* You can't change the fact that highly stressful events happen, but you can change how you interpret and respond to these events.
- *accepting that change is a part of living.*
- *moving toward your goals.* Develop some realistic goals. Do something regularly – even if it seems like a small accomplishment – that enables you to move toward your goals.
- *taking decisive actions.* Act on adverse situations as much as you can. Take decisive actions, rather than detaching completely from problems and stresses and wishing they would just go away.
- *looking for opportunities for self-discovery.* People often learn something about themselves and may find that they have grown in some respect as a result of their struggle with loss.
- *nurturing a positive view of yourself.* Developing confidence in your ability to solve problems and trusting your instincts helps build resilience.

- *keeping things in perspective.* Even when facing very painful events, try to consider the stressful situation in a broader context and keep a long-term perspective. Avoid blowing the event out of proportion.

- *maintain a hopeful outlook.* An optimistic outlook enables you to expect that good things will happen in your life. Try visualising what you want, rather than worrying about what you fear.

- *taking care of yourself.* Pay attention to your own needs and feelings. Engage in activities that you enjoy and find relaxing. Exercise regularly. Taking care of yourself helps to keep your mind and body primed to deal with situations that require resilience.

The key is to identify ways that are likely to work well for you as part of your own personal strategy for fostering resilience.

In their groundbreaking book, *The Power of Full Engagement*, Jim Loehr and Tony Schwartz [29] suggest getting more done in your life (with higher levels of satisfaction) is not about managing time, *it's about managing your energy.* There are four sources of energy: *physical, emotional, mental and spiritual.* With each source, we must find a way to balance energy use and energy renewal. When any energy source is out of balance we become burned out and our performance suffers.

To change this, we must increase the capacity of each energy source by pushing beyond our normal limits and then renew the source with a corresponding rest period. It's exactly the way we increase our physical strength. We work out a muscle to exhaustion and then we rest it. The exertion and rest period makes the muscle stronger. We need to be able to balance the degree of work and rest – but too much rest means the muscle will atrophy.

In our ever increasingly busy lives, finding – or more accurately creating – periods of rest or "down time" seems difficult. Just as cleaning our teeth is a ritual developed over time, we equally need to create positive energy rituals in our lives. Rituals are specific routines that we do without even thinking about them.

The number of hours in a day is fixed, but the *quantity* and *quality* of energy available to us is not. This fundamental insight has the power to revolutionise the way we live our lives. In order to build resilience and build our capability to not just "cope" with what life throws at us, we need to do be able to do four things:

- *Mobilise* four key sources of energy.
- *Balance* energy expenditure with intermittent energy renewal.
- *Expand* capacity in the same systematic way that elite athletes do.
- *Create* highly specific, positive energy management rituals.

Now back to Robert. After a fairly lengthy conversation which touched a number of areas, he could see a glimmer of hope. He could see that he was not a victim of circumstance and could actually change his life for the better – and importantly, he now could see that his choices and way of seeing things had created the world he now called his life.

Building your 'resilient muscle' is an individual experience. Adapt these tips for your own situation, keeping in mind what has and has not worked for you in the past.

Importantly, Robert engaged those around him to get involved and also for support. Many of us feel exactly the same way Robert did, but instead of sharing it, we choose to keep it to ourselves because that's what everyone else does.

Focusing more on enhancing our physical, emotional, mental and spiritual (purpose and meaning) capabilities will pay huge dividends. It'll enable you to develop a reservoir of internal resources that you can draw on, allowing you to not just to cope with life, but thrive and prosper. Applying the principles of positive psychology and strengths-based leadership can also make a big difference. Anything else is selling yourself, and those who care about you, short. *And frankly, you're worth* it.

Chapter 17

You

Robert was struggling to communicate a vision or strategy for API. We have already discussed his lack of authenticity and failure to connect with people in a meaningful way or influence them effectively. If Robert and his executive team weren't really connected to the mission, vision and values, how could they expect others to be?

Leadership comes from a deeper reality – it comes from our *values, principles, life experiences and essence.* It is a *whole-of-person* action. Character is the essence of a leader and works to transform and open up possibilities and potential.

Robert and many of his team instead came from a pattern of coping, where they tended to react to circumstances to elicit an immediate result. Coping leaders are often defensive, controlling, aggressive, have a "win-lose" mentality and resist change. Many of these negative attributes are driven by self-limiting beliefs. "If I don't act in an authoritative way people won't do what they're supposed to," or "I have to know the answer to appear credible," or "I like to challenge and show the holes in people's arguments." The exploration of beliefs and taking people through a process to deepen each person's understanding of their "world view" is often transformational.

Robert and the team eventually engaged some outside support to develop their leadership capability in the area of character and mastery. Some of the things they worked on were:

- learning to take *full* responsibility for outcomes.
- raising awareness of their individual and collective beliefs and working through the limiting beliefs.
- developing strategies to lead and live through their character (rather than coping mechanisms).
- learning how to support each other, including "calling" behaviours which were dysfunctional, and
- gaining a sense of purposefulness, both individually and as a team.

After several months of "working on themselves", there was a renewed sense of energy and clarity around the mission, vision and values. They had learned how to have robust, crucial conversations. Levels of trust had improved, although actions speak louder than words so this will take more time. Relationships within the team had improved markedly and progress had been made outside the team. There was a sense of purpose that was being felt right throughout API. They had learned how to tell a "turnaround story" that engaged and energised the workforce.

Robert and the team had learned some key principles around adaptive leadership and were starting to empower individuals, teams and business units to make progress on their toughest challenges. Change was being managed and led in a systemic and thoughtful way. This had freed up the executive team to focus on strategic leadership and remove the organisation-wide impediments to progress.

Robert also noticed that his energy had returned and he was feeling optimistic about the future. He noticed that relationships at work felt much easier and even enjoyable again. Importantly, API started to show substantial improvements in innovation and collaboration, and performance was improving. The organisation had stopped hemorrhaging and was on the road to recovery.

Chapter 18

What to do with this Leadership Declaration

The aim of writing this book – particularly our Leadership Declaration – is to inspire and ignite leadership action that makes a difference for you, your organisation and the world we live in.

Its purpose is to clearly state the case for leadership and its importance to all of us at this time. At an organisational level, there is little doubt that *real* leadership is the 'engine room' of performance. In the absence of systemic, results-focused leadership, breakthrough performance and high commitment will not be achieved.

To make progress on our most significant issues, I believe that we need a new paradigm of leadership that supersedes the outdated industrial age leadership paradigm and liberates us from old ways of thinking about how to manage and lead people. A new paradigm needs to guide our actions and decisions in a constructive, values-driven way. It is one that will empower each of us to take full responsibility and accountability at all levels of organisations, in government, and in the community. Importantly, a new paradigm will create an environment of high levels of commitment and learning.

A new paradigm creates enormous possibility for organisations and the societies in which we live. The limits to human potential and ingenuity have barely been tested. A new paradigm holds the promise of at least elevating our chances of creating more humanistic, inspiring places for people to innovate and produce products and services that will *create breakthrough performance* and make a difference.

We are interested in developing leaders from many different industries, fields and walks of life. We have had the privilege over many years to come into contact with some wonderful leaders – the men and women who are able to continually meet or exceed performance expectations while having the wonderful ability to draw forth the great potential of those around them.

If you find the ideas in this book enticing, or your find that you are already aligned to a new leadership paradigm as discussed, here's what you can do:

- Generate a conversation with you colleagues about the ideas in this book and see what they think.
- Visit www.leadershipwithoutsilverbullets.com.au and participate in the online discussion forum, access additional resources, or order additional copies.
- Send us an email with your thoughts on *Leadership Without Silver Bullets.*
- Invite people to a brown paper bag lunch meeting where you will discuss this book and the new leadership paradigm.
- Take a stand for leadership and leadership development in your organisation. If you need help in bringing a leadership development focus to your organisation, please call us for a free consultation.

If you would like more information on how The Leadership Sphere can help you improve the leadership capability in your organisation to deliver breakthrough performance, please contact:

info@theleadershipsphere.com.au

www.theleadershipsphere.com.au

Order copies at: http://www.leadershipwithoutsilverbullets.com.au

About the Author

Phillip Ralph is a leading consultant to CEOs and executives and he partners with organisations to achieve breakthrough leadership, team and organisational performance. He is an author, coach, facilitator and keynote speaker. Phillip is the founder of the consultancy firm, *The Leadership Sphere*.

His areas of expertise are leadership development, team development and cultural transformation to enable clients to achieve their strategic goals. Phillip has twenty years experience working with a diverse number of clients in Australia and internationally. The proprietary methodology employed by TLS integrates a systems view *with* a whole-of-person approach, supported by a diverse range of commercial, government and senior corporate experience.

Phillip's clients are predominately ASX200 organisations (or equivalent private firms) in diverse industries including banking and finance; legal, accounting and consulting firms; industrial companies, health, as well as not-for-profits. He works with CEOs and executives as an executive coach and facilitates several innovative leadership development programs. His experience includes working with McKinsey & Co, focusing on leadership development and building relationship and consulting skills for large professional services firms.

Prior to founding The Leadership Sphere, Phillip spent six years with the highly successful and innovative ANZ cultural transformation program called Breakout, where he was the Head of Consulting and Program Delivery. *Breakout* has been widely acclaimed as one of the best examples of a successful cultural transformation program in the world.

Phillip resides in Melbourne, Australia with his wife Kerrie and three children (14,14, and 10 years old). His hobbies include keeping fit by jogging and cycling, vicariously participating in many sports, reading, aviation and dining.

Contact/Organisation details

The Leadership Sphere was formed in 2007 by Phillip Ralph and Associates, who have a long history of supporting organisations to create *breakthrough performance*. The Leadership Sphere (TLS) partners with organisations to achieve sustainable high performance through a powerful multi-disciplinary approach, focusing in the areas of leadership development, team development and cultural transformation. Our point of difference is a structured systemic approach to achieve realistic and sustainable positive change leading to *breakthrough performance*.

Our prestigious clients include a wide range of major companies across the public sector and private industry, many of whom are Top 100 ASX companies. We have services in all states of Australia and in the United States, the United Kingdom, New Zealand, Hong Kong, Singapore, Spain and the Netherlands.

Why Do We Do What We Do?
We do what we do for one simple, yet compelling reason – and that is our strong desire to see every individual, team and organisation unlock the potential and energy that will make all the difference.

Who do we work with?

- Managing Directors and CEOs.

- Senior executives.

- Leaders.

- High potential/fast track employees.

- Leaders in transition.

- Organisations that want high performance cultures (including increasing engagement).

- Teams who have a desire to excel.

We work with senior leaders and teams at the intrapersonal, interpersonal and group levels. By working at multiple levels, we are able to help our clients achieve significant shifts that stick.

We are renowned in the marketplace for the following:

- The desired change happens (individual, team and organisational transformation).

- We have a transparent business model. There is a clear scope of work and costs.

- We deliver what we say we're going to deliver.

Our Values

Our values are important to us. These are the non-negotiable minimum standards to which all our work and dealings apply. These values are not a high aspiration we strive for, but rather the way we do business. When we are true to our values, our clients know it.

Customer

Being the best for our clients means a customer-driven approach rather than a provider or product driven approach. This may seem pedantic, but it makes all the difference. Many consultants and coaches start with their paradigm or framework and fit that to their clients rather than other way around. At TLS, we work back from the client's needs and customise the approach to optimise outcomes.

Partnership

We adopt a partnering approach for several reasons. Firstly, we prefer that our clients have energy and buy-in around the reasons we were hired in the first place. The desired change will simply not be self-sustaining otherwise. Secondly, we consciously work to transfer skill and knowledge where applicable. This helps ensure a system which is self-reinforcing and sustaining. Thirdly, it is more enjoyable for both us and the clients when we work together to solve problems.

Ethical Practice

Ethical practice means never compromising our own integrity or that of our clients. Again, many consultants and coaches collude with the client system by "selling in" products and services that don't address the true underlying issues. While we can provide you or your people with off-the-shelf products, we will always alert you to the pros and cons. Practicing in an ethical manner means that we work in the best interests of our clients, not us.

Leadership

Leadership to us means being at the forefront of the latest thinking from around the world so we can bring the best to our clients. It is also reflected in how we engage with all our stakeholders, be they clients, suppliers, government or our own people. We believe that we can make a powerful difference in the world, both through leaders and by being leaders. Making a difference means enabling people to be all they can be, regardless of the organisation, culture, gender, race or age. The bottom line is people living more fulfilling lives in a sustainable way.

Courage

Being courageous comes in many forms. For us, however, it means being bold and different as consultants. It means doing things differently from the pack – creating value beyond the norm by putting ourselves out there. Our consultants and coaches need to demonstrate and model the behaviours that we ask of our clients, whether they are a senior leader or a team that feels stuck. We need to be prepared to go to the hard places to help our clients.

Excellence

It means striving to be the best in whatever we do, not so we can say we're the best compared to others, but so we can say we were the best for our client. It also means having the best people working for us. Our clients rightly expect work of the highest quality – accurate, valuable, on time, on budget and with no surprises.

Community

We have a strong sense of doing what is right for the community and feel a responsibility to all people. We have a desire for a world that is peaceful, equitable and where people are honest with one another. We value spouses, children and family. We want everyone to have the opportunity to grow and be the best they can be, whatever this means for them.

The Leadership Sphere Pty Ltd
Level 23, HWT Tower, 40 City Road
Southgate, Victoria, 3006, Australia

info@theleadershipsphere.com.au

www.theleadershipsphere.com.au

If you would like to purchase additional copies, please   visit www.leadershipwithoutsilverbullets.com.au.

Useful Resources

Buckingham, M (2007). *Go Put Your Strengths to Work: 6 Powerful Steps to Achieve Outstanding Performance.* New York: One Thing Productions.

Brookfields, SD (1991). *Developing Critical Thinkers.* Oxford: Jossey-Bass Publishers.

Cashman, K (2003). *Awakening the Leader Within: A Story of Transformation.* New Jersey: John Wiley & Sons, Inc.

Camillus, JC (2008). "Strategy as a Wicked Problem", *Harvard Business Review.*

Covey, S (2004). *The 8th Habit: From Effectiveness to Greatness* New York: Free Press.

Crum, TF, & Denver J (1987). *The Magic of Conflict: Turning Life of Work into a Work of Art.* New York: Rockefeller Centre.

Csikszentmihalyi, M (2000). "The Contribution of Flow to Positive Psychology" *in The Science of Optimism and Hope.* Ed. J.E. Gillham, 387-395. Radnor, PA: Templeton Foundation Press.

Gallwey WT (2003). *The Inner Game of Work: Overcoming Mental Obstacles for Maximum Performance.* London: Random House.

Gardner, H (2004). *Changing Minds.* Boston: Harvard Business School Press.

Gladwell, M (2005). *Blink.* Sydney: Allen Lane (Penguin Group).

Goleman, D (2006). *Social Intelligence – The New Science of Human Relationships.* London: Hutchinson.

Goleman D (2003). *Destructive Emotions and How We Can Overcome Them.* Great Britain: Batman Books.

Greenleaf, RK (1991). *Servant Leadership.* New York: Paulist Press, New York.

Heifetz, RA, & Linsky, M (2002). "A survival guide for leaders", *Harvard Business Review.*

Heifetz, RA, & Laurie, DL (2002). "The Work of Leadership", *Harvard Business Review.*

Goleman, D, (1998). "What Makes a Leader?", *Harvard Business Review.*

Kegan R, & Lahey LL (2009). *Immunity to Change: How to Overcome it and Unlock the Potential in Yourself and Your Organization.* Boston: Harvard Business School.

Keith, K (2006). *Engagement is Not Enough: You Need Passionate Employees to Achieve Your Dream.* San Diego: Advantage Publishing.

Kouzes, J (2003). *Business Leadership.* San Francisco: Jossey-Bass.

Lee, G (2003). *Leadership Coaching.* London: CIPD (Chartered Institute of Personnel Development).

Levitt, SD & Dubner, SJ (2005). *Freakonomics.* Melbourne: Penguin Books Ltd.

Linley, AP & Joseph, S (Ed.) (2004). *Positive Psychology in Practice.* New Jersey: John Wiley and Sons.

Maister, DH Green, CH, Galford, R.M. (2000). *The Trusted Advisor.* New York: Free Press.

Malandro, L (2003). *Say it Right, The First Time.* New York: McGraw-Hill.

Martin, R, (2007). "Choices, Conflict, and the Creative Spark. The Problem-Solving Power of Integrative Thinking", Excerpted from *The Opposable Mind: How Successful Leaders Win Through Integrative Thinking,* Harvard Business Press.

Parashar, F (2003). *The Balancing Act: Work-Life Solutions for Busy People.* Sydney: Simon & Schuster.

Patterson, K, Grenny, J, McMillan, R., Switzler A., (2002). *Crucial Conversations: Tools for Talking Tough When Stakes are High.* New York: McGraw-Hill.

Pink, D (2006). *A Whole New Mind: Why Right-Brainers Will Rule the Future.* Riverhead Trade.

Seligman, EP (2004). *Character Strengths and Virtues: A Handbook and Classification.* Oxford University Press.

Ray, M (2005). *The Highest Goal: The Secret That Sustains You In Every Moment.* San Francisco: Berrett-Koehler.

Pfeffer, J (1998). *Human Equation: Building Profits by Putting People First.* Boston: Harvard Business School Press.

Scott S (2002). *Fierce Conversations: Achieving Success in Work and in Life, One Conversation at a Time.* London: Judy Piatkus (Publishers) Limited.

Seligman, EP (2002). *Authentic Happiness – Using the New Positive Psychology to Realize Your Potential for Lasting Fulfillment.* Random House: Sydney.

Senge, P, Sharmer, CO, Jaworski, J, Flowers, BS (2004). *Presence: Human Purpose and the Field of the Future.* Massachusetts: The Society for Organizational Learning.

Snyder, CR, & Lopez, SJ (2007). *Positive Psychology – The Scientific and Practical Explorations of Human Strengths.* London: Sage Publications.

Stober DR, & Grant AM (Eds)., (2006). *Evidence Based Coaching Handbook.* United States: John Wiley & Sons.

Wageman, R., Nunes, DA, Burruss, JA, Hackman, JR (2008). *Senior Leadership Teams: What it Takes to Make them Great.* Boston: Harvard Business School Publishing.

Whitmore J (2002). *Coaching for Performance: Growing People, Performance and Purpose.* London: WS Bookwell.

On-line Resources

The Australian Leadership Blog
www.theaustralianleadershipblog.com.au

The Benevolent Society/Social Leadership Australia
www.bensoc.org.au

Harvard Business Review
www.hbr.org

Human Synergistics
www.human-synergistics.com.au
www.leadinghs.com.au

McKinsey Quarterly
www.mckinseyquarterly.com

Ted – a not-for-profit site dedicated to Ideas Worth Spreading
www.ted.com

The Leadership Sphere
www.theleadershipsphere.com.au

University of Pennsylvania - Authentic Happiness
www.authentichappiness.sas.upenn.edu

University of Pennsylvania - Positive Psychology Centre
www.ppc.sas.upenn.edu

Partners

Callahan Associates, Singapore
www.callahan-asc.com

Crossroads Human Resources
www.crossroadshr.com.au

Organisational Storytelling
www.onethousandandone.com.au

Teamscape
www.teamscape.com.au

Bibliography

1. Picknett, L, Prince, C, Prior, S and Brydon, R. *War of the Windsors: A Century of Unconstitutional Monarchy.* s.l. : Mainstream Publishing, 2002.
2. Wagner, Kendra Van. Leadership Theories. *about.com (psychology).* [Online] 2009. http://psychology.about.com/od/leadership/p/leadtheories.htm.
3. Covey, S. Leading in the Knowledge Worker Age. [ed.] M & Hesselbein, F Goldsmith. *The Leader of the Future: Visions, Strategies, and Practices for the New Era.* San Francisco : Jossey-Bass, 2006.
4. Hower, M. Leadership & Systematic Change: Making a New Paradigm As We Go. *Antioch University - Centre for Creative Change.* [Online] http://www.antiochsea.edu/academics/enviro/faculty/Hower_Mark.html.
5. Rost, J. *Leadership for the 21st Century.* Westport : Praeger Publishers, 1993.
6. —. Moving from Individual to Relationship: A Postindustrial Paradigm of Leadership. *Journal of Leadership and Organisational Studies.* 1997, Vol. 4.
7. Hock, D. *Birth of the Chaordic Age.* San Francisco : Berrett-Koelher, 1999.
8. Handy, C. Philosopher Leaders. [ed.] F & Hasselbein, M & Beckhard, R Goldsmith. *The Leader of the Future: Visions, Strategies and Practices for the New Era.* San Francisco : Jossey-Bass, 2006.
9. Deutschman, A. Change or Die. *Fast Company.* [Online] http://www.fastcompany.com.
10. Williams, D. *Real Leadership: Helping People and Organizations Face Their Toughest Challenges.* San Francisco : Berrett-Koehler, 2005.
11. Heifetz, R Grashow, A & Linsky, M. *The Practice of Adaptive Leadership - Tools and Tactics for Changing Your Organization and the World.* Boston, Massachusetts : Harvard Business Press, 2009.
12. Gerzon, M. Leaders & Leadership. [Online] September 2003. http://www.beyondintractability.org.
13. *Edelman Trust Barometer Executive Summary.* Edelman, R. New York : Richard Edelman, 2009.

144

14. United Nations. *The 2nd UN World Water Development Report: 'Water, A Shared Responsibility'.* Prague : United Nations, March, 2006.
15. World Bank. World Bank Updates Poverty Estimates for the Developing World. *www.worldbank.org.*
   [Online] December 30, 2008. http://econ.worldbank.org.
16. D, Clark. The Art & Science of Leadership. *www.nwlink.com.* [Online]
17. Beer, M. *High Commitment High Performance - How to Build a Resilient Organization for Sustained Advantage.* San Francisco : John Wiley & Sons, 2009.
18. De Geus, A. *Planning as Learning.* March-April, 1988, Harvard Business Review, Vols. 74-78.
19. Burns, JM. *Leadership.* New York : Harper, 1978.
20. Hollander, EP. *Leadership Dynamics: A Practical Guide to Effective Relationships.* New York : Free Press, 1992.
21. Heifetz, R & Linsky, M. *Leadership on the Line: Staying Alive through the Dangers of Leading.* Boston : Harvard Business School Press, 2002.
22. Heifetz, RA. *Leadership vs Authority.* 1999. Vol. 36 & 19.
23. Heifetz, R and Laurie, O. The Work of Leadership. *Harvard Business Review.* 1997, January.
24. Leadership Theories. *www.changingminds.org.* [Online] 2009.
25. Cashman, K. *Leadership from the Inside Out.* San Francisco : Berrett-Koehler Publishers Inc, 2008.
26. Schein, E. Leadership Competencies: A Provocative New Look. [ed.] M, Hasselbein, F & Beckhard R Goldsmith. *The Leader of the Future: Visions, Strategies and Practices for the New Era.* San Francisco : Jossey-Bass, 2006.
27. Wortmann, C. *What's Your Story: Using Stories to Ignite Performance and Be More Successful.* Chicago : Kaplan Publishing, 2006.
28. American Psychological Society. Resilience. *www.apa.org.*
   [Online] January 2010.
29. Loehr, J & Schwartz, T. *The Power of Full Engagement.* New York : Free Press, 2003.

Index